"An excellent book about a traumatic topic. Ken Blue puts his finger on some very real problems and offers sensible solutions. I strongly recommend this book."

IRVING HEXHAM
professor of religious studies, University of Calgary

"For the soul that still aches from being used or abused by a minister or a ministry, there is hope for healing in *Healing Spiritual Abuse*. Once you've figured out you've been a victim of spiritual abuse, reading this book is the next step toward a renewed relationship with Christ."

STEPHEN ARTERBURN
New Life Treatment Centers

"The evil Ken Blue writes about is real, widespread and deadly. It produces similar effects in Christians to those that battering husbands have on their beat-up wives (if they do not leave the batterer, hope dies, and with it every spark of vitality). Happily, Ken understands the solutions and points to them clearly."

JOHN WHITE
author

"With the kind of biblical insight and pastoral wisdom we have come to expect of Ken Blue, this book probes the conscience of those who unknowingly practice spiritual abuse by contrasting Jesus' empowering ministry to others with a Pharisaical exploitation of others in order to gain power. For those who have been and are the victims of spiritual abuse under the cover of ecclesial office and authority, reading this book will open windows to freedom and healing."

RAY ANDERSON
professor of theology and ministry,
Fuller Theological Seminary

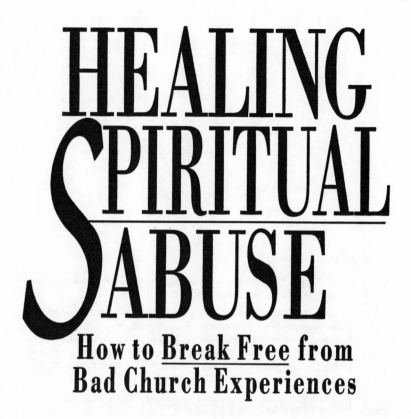

HEALING SPIRITUAL ABUSE

How to Break Free from Bad Church Experiences

Ken Blue

INTERVARSITY PRESS
DOWNERS GROVE, ILLINOIS 60515

127135

InterVarsity Press® is the book-publishing division of InterVarsity Christian Fellowship®, a student movement active on campus at hundreds of universities, colleges and schools of nursing in the United States of America, and a member movement of the International Fellowship of Evangelical Students. For information about local and regional activities, write Public Relations Dept., InterVarsity Christian Fellowship, 6400 Schroeder Rd., P.O. Box 7895, Madison, WI 53707-7895.

All Scripture quotations, unless otherwise indicated, are from the HOLY BIBLE, NEW INTERNATIONAL VERSION®. NIV®. Copyright ©1973, 1978, 1984 by International Bible Society. Used by permission of Zondervan Publishing House. All rights reserved.

ISBN 0-8308-1660-7

Printed in the United States of America ∞

Library of Congress Cataloging-in-Publication Data
Blue, Ken, 1945-
    Healing spiritual abuse: how to break free from bad church experiences/Ken Blue.
        p.   cm.
    Includes bibliographical references.
    ISBN 0-8308-1660-7
    1. religious addiction. 2. Christianity—Psychology.
3. Christian leadership. 4. Manipulative behavior. 5. Bible.   N.T.
Matthew—Criticism, interpretation, etc.   I. Title.
BR114.B584   1993
248.8'6—dc20   93-21558
                                                                              CIP

15	14	13	12	11	10	9	8	7	6	5	4	3	2	1
04	03	02	01	00	99	98	97	96	95	94	93			

To all those
who trusted me
with their stories

Acknowledgments

I am grateful first to my secretary, Wendy Paris, who prepared this manuscript and offered encouragement. My thanks also to Patti, my wife of twenty years, and our children, Aaron, Emmet, Mason, Wayland, Kallee, Levi and Ana, for giving me space to work. My appreciation to my brothers and sisters at Foothills Church in San Diego, California, who sustained me in this effort. Finally, I wish to thank David Johnson, pastor of Church of the Open Door in Crystal, Minnesota. His teaching on spiritual abuse broke the ground for much of my own thinking on this issue.

Men never do evil so completely and cheerfully as when they do it from religious conviction.
Pascal

You will know the truth, and the truth will set you free.
Jesus Christ

It is for freedom that Christ has set us free. Stand firm, then, and do not let yourselves be burdened again by a yoke of slavery.
The apostle Paul

1
AN INVITATION TO FREEDOM

A *televangelist is tried, convicted* and sent to jail for defrauding his followers. A well-known pastor admits to extorting sex from his female staff. The Roman Catholic Church spends millions on out-of-court settlements to those who claim to have been sexually molested by priests. A young woman commits suicide after her pastor says she is demon-possessed and there is no hope for her. A prominent Christian leader writes a book calling for integrity in ministry and then is exposed as an adulterer. A four-year-old boy dies for lack of a lifesaving medical procedure; his parents' pastor insisted they not call a doctor but depend on prayer alone. Several couples in a small rural church divorce because the minister says their marriages are outside God's perfect will. The ministry credentials of a prominent theologian and ethicist are suspended after numerous female coleaders accuse him of sexual misconduct.

These are just a few examples of a contemporary problem people are calling "spiritual abuse." Actually, spiritual abuse has been a problem for the people of God from the start.[1] The term itself, however, is relatively new.[2] Trendy and provocative terms such as *spiritual abuse* soon lose meaning through overuse or misuse. So let's begin with some careful definitions: What is spiritual abuse? What kind of person abuses spiritually? What effect does this abuse have on its victims?

What Is It, and Who Does It?

Abuse of any type occurs when someone has power over another and uses that power to hurt. Physical abuse means that someone exercises physical power over another, causing physical wounds. Sexual abuse means that someone exercises sexual power over another, resulting in sexual wounds. And spiritual abuse happens when a leader with spiritual authority uses that authority to coerce, control or exploit a follower, thus causing spiritual wounds. Ron Enroth explains further:

> Unlike physical abuse that often results in bruised bodies, spiritual and pastoral abuse leaves scars on the psyche and soul. It is inflicted by persons who are accorded respect and honor in our society by virtue of their role as religious leaders and models of spiritual authority. They base that authority on the Bible, the Word of God, and see themselves as shepherds with a sacred trust. But when they violate that trust, when they abuse their authority and when they misuse ecclesiastical power to control and manipulate the flock, the results can be catastrophic.[3]

Spiritual abuse may differ from some other forms of abuse in that it is rarely perpetrated with intent to maim. As we shall see, spiritual abusers are curiously naive about the effects of their exploitation. They rarely intend to hurt their victims. They are usually so narcissistic or so focused on some great thing they are doing for God that they don't notice the wounds they are inflicting on their followers. So though I maintain that spiritual abuse is evil and dangerous and must be stopped, my definition of it leaves out the term *intent to hurt.*

And the definition needs to be limited even more. Think of spiritual abuse on a vertical continuum: minor, sporadic abuse belongs at the bottom end of the spectrum, with heavy-handed and systematic abuse at the top. Mere thoughtlessness, rudeness and arrogance among those in church leadership are not my concern in this book. If everything church leaders do wrong is called spiritual abuse, the issue is trivialized. I want to discourage the superficial labeling of too many pastors as spiritual abusers. Let's deal responsibly with the real problem and not turn our concern with spiritual abuse into the Salem witch hunt of our time.

Given these cautions, we must still be discerning. Some very pleasant and socially acceptable behavior is nevertheless calculated to manipulate and so is abusive.

Some spiritual leaders gently coerce their congregations through skillful use of the language of intimacy and trust. This same technique of subtle manipulation is evident in upscale restaurants. Servers in these restaurants are well trained in the vocabulary and body language of friendliness and familiarity. By the proper use of key words, touches and gestures, the server gains the customer's trust. He or she then plays on this trust, manipulating the customer into ordering what the restaurant wants to sell rather than what the customer wants to eat. The purpose is to extract the greatest amount of money while making the customer feel loved and cared for.

Many church leaders are skilled in this language of intimacy and trust. With it they gain the support of their followers and are able to run the church as they please. In light of the serious trauma caused by heavy-handed abusers, such subtle manipulation may seem quite minor. It is significant, however, because it is a violation of trust. When a leader pretends to be a friend and uses this illusion to dehumanize and manipulate his followers, he is acting abusively. So I will place such behavior on the continuum of spiritual abuse, toward the bottom.

At the top end of the continuum I place the deliberate exploitation and domination of the weak by a grandiose, authoritarian spiritual dictator. Almost any kind of abusive behavior may be found at this level: threats, intimidation, extortion of money, demands for sex, public humiliation, control over private lives, manipulation of marriages, elaborate spying and similar practices. When psychologically and spiritually weak people fall under the control of a narcissistic demagogue, there is potential for great harm to all. The examples of spiritual abuse I use in this book fall somewhere on the spectrum between significant but minor abuse to extreme abuse.[4]

Who Are the Victims?

More than twenty years ago—one week after beginning my first pastoral assignment—I was called to the local hospital. One of my parishioners (a twenty-five-year-old woman whom I will call Martha[5]) had attempted suicide and was recovering in intensive care. Our initial conversation was painfully awkward—not just because this was our first meeting, or because I was a "rookie" on a difficult assignment, but because Martha was terrified of me. When I realized this, I asked her why she was afraid. Her reply came in a low, almost menacing voice, "Because you are a minister."

I asked her to explain what she meant, but she turned away without answering. After a long, uncomfortable silence, I asked if I could read some Scriptures to her. Martha was quiet for a moment and then (with her back still turned) said, "Please don't. I'm not strong enough for that."

Thoroughly confused and demoralized, I excused myself and left the room.

In the following months Martha and I became friends, and she told me her story. She was born into a fundamentalist Christian home and raised in a religiously conservative farming community. Her parents used God and the Bible to threaten and control her. God was always pictured as a severe judge who demanded perfection in thought and deed. Since she fell short of this standard, she constantly feared his punishment. When her pet calf died of colic, Martha believed God was punishing her for some sin.

As Martha grew up, she found that she not only was afraid of God but also feared anything related to him. She became agitated and uncomfortable in the presence of a pastor and couldn't read any part of the Bible without feeling physically ill. After graduating from nursing school in her mid-twenties, Martha became seriously depressed. Seeking comfort in a sexual relationship with a married man, she became pregnant. In despair, feeling that God was now punishing her for her sin, she attempted suicide.

Years after Martha's attempt on her own life, and after many hours of skilled counseling and loving pastoral care, Martha is doing well. Some time ago I asked her how she was and she replied, "Well, I can look you in the face and speak to you without shaking. I can read my Bible without getting sick. And I can come to church without my stomach tying up in knots. I'm doing great!"

People who "survive" spiritual abuse often wander in a kind of limbo; they are confused, hurt and angry. Some victims of pastoral abuse blame themselves for their suffering, thinking that they must have deserved it. Others indulge in self-hate for foolishly submitting themselves and their families to such humiliation. Others focus their hatred on the abuser. They are soon crippled by bitterness and cut off from God's healing. As Juanita and Dale Ryan say, "Spiritual abuse is a kind of abuse which damages the central core of who we are. It leaves us spiritually disorganized and emotionally cut off from the healing love of God."[6]

Most victims of spiritual abuse are loners. However, sometimes they band together with others who share their experience. Fifteen such people descended on a church I once served. They had all spent the previous years together in a congregation associated with the so-called discipleship/shepherding movement.[7] Each of them had wanted to leave this church for some time but were emotionally unable to go it alone. They finally banded together and departed en masse.

During their first year with us, I heard each of their stories. They painted a consistent picture of their former church. It was rigidly hierarchical. Every member was assigned to a personal pastor who ruled over their lives much as a parent supervises preadolescent children. Each personal pastor told his followers what profession to follow, what car to buy, where to go on vacation and the like. The personal pastor decided how many children a couple should have and how they should be raised. Members of this church gave up all significant decision-making and eventually any sense of personal autonomy and identity.

I asked several of them why they willingly participated in their own dehumanization. "After all," I said, "no one held a gun to your head." Their response was uniform. They each said they had believed the way they were being treated was right, and that in the end they would be rewarded for their loyalty and submission.

The hierarchical structure of their group was not only oppressive but also addictive. Most of these people became so habituated to rigid accountability that when they finally left the abusing church they felt utterly lost. Every one of them became depressed, some severely. Years later, many have yet to recover. Some of them turned to alcohol and prescription drugs for relief. Several of the marriages became abusive. Men who had been highly motivated, productive professionals prior to their involvement in the shepherding group couldn't hold a job after they left it.

As I listened to each story, I was struck by how intensely dedicated to Christ they all had been at one time. In the beginning each wanted his or her life to count for the kingdom of God. It was this eagerness to "sell out for Jesus" that made the shepherding church so attractive to them originally. This church held up the call to a higher, nobler, more sacrificial brand of discipleship. Because they were long on enthusiasm and short on wisdom, these eager disciples soon became victims of spiritual abuse.

As we shall see, the most committed believers are often the most vulnerable to abusive religion. But as the Berks say, "The Gospel means life to those who are spiritually dead. The Shepherding movement has increasingly brought spiritual death to those who were once spiritually alive."[8]

Is There Freedom from Abuse?

In over twenty years of public ministry, I have collected many stories of spiritual abuse. The abundance and prevalence of such experiences gradually led me to believe that the problem of powerful Christians hurting weaker brothers and sisters was more or less inevitable.

Not long ago, however, my pessimistic and passive attitude toward this issue changed radically and almost instantaneously while I was preparing a sermon. I had been preaching from the Gospel of Matthew. As I came to the twenty-third chapter where Jesus publicly confronts the Pharisees about the dereliction of their pastoral duties, I was tempted to skip those verses because they seemed to have little relevance for the pastoral needs of my congregation. Then, as if seeing for the first time what Jesus was saying, I realized that the authoritarian, narcissistic ecclesiastical abusers of our day are the modern equivalent of the Pharisees whom Jesus scolded. Jesus not only exposed and denounced the Pharisees as false shepherds but also offered himself as advocate for their victims. His teaching in Matthew 23 gives hope and instruction to all those hurt by pastoral abuse.

Jesus did not resign himself to spiritual abuse. He stood up to it.

He demanded change. Why should we do less?

Once I saw what Jesus was really saying in Matthew 23, I found him saying similar things throughout the Gospels. In fact, Jesus was so focused on the problem of spiritual abuse that it was the only social evil against which he ever developed a platform. It was the only cultural problem that he repeatedly exposed and opposed. This is amazing when we recall that his culture was plagued by a host of serious social ills. Jesus took no public stand against slavery, racism, class warfare, state-sponsored terrorism, military occupation or corruption in government. He spoke not a word against abortion or infanticide, homosexuality or the exploitation of women and children. All of these and more were pressing problems in Jesus' day, but we have no record of his directly addressing them.

The modern church *has* spoken out against each of these social ills. Surprisingly, however, until recently we have said virtually nothing about spiritual abuse, the one social problem Jesus himself seemed to care about most.

Instead of skipping Matthew 23 as irrelevant, I preached a series of sermons from it. The response to those sermons (and the tape series containing them) was overwhelming! Dozens of people from the congregation brought me not only their stories of previous spiritual abuse but those of their friends and family. The spiritually abused and abusers began to understand their experiences in a fresh light, forgave (or repented) and received the forgiveness of Jesus and his church. Many reported feelings of intense freedom and joy.

Wherever I travel for ministry conferences, I am amazed at the multitude of stories of spiritual abuse which people now seem eager to share. Church of England bishops, rural Romanian peasants, South African politicians—all have told stories of abuse and manipulation. And in all cases and cultures, the principles Jesus taught (as recorded in Matthew 23) hold the key to healing and wholeness today, just they did for the Pharisees and their victims.

Looking Ahead

The next five chapters of this book are an exposition and application of Matthew 23. In chapter two we'll see how Jesus exposes the illegitimate means by which the Pharisees initially gained control over the people: they took for themselves the exalted "seat of Moses." They said, in effect, "Because we speak for Moses [who spoke for God], you must obey us." The modern equivalent of this is the church leader who says, "Because I am 'the Lord's anointed,' or the pastor, or the elder, or the bishop, you must do as I say." Jesus and Paul make very clear, however, that no office, position or title automatically carries with it any spiritual authority. The only true authority in the kingdom of God comes through servant leadership.

We find in chapter three that it was not just the Pharisees' false authority that made them dangerous but also their false teaching. They taught a false view of God and a false way of serving him. They pictured God as a legalistic judge, favoring those who kept his religious rules and despising those who did not. Modern preachers who make God's acceptance contingent upon religious performance are the Pharisees of today. Jesus says, in effect, that high-sounding religious lies spoken by respected leaders are ruinous to spiritual life.

Jesus tells us how to spot false teachers, and this is the subject of chapter four. He says they lay heavy religious burdens on men and women but do not lift a finger to move them. These burdens are laws and regulations that appear to be spiritual but actually paralyze spiritual growth. Evangelical, fundamentalist and Roman Catholic legalisms are today's heavy loads. And those who pile them on people are the same as the Pharisees Jesus denounced in his day. Good shepherds lift these burdens off, setting followers free.

In chapter five we discover that the abusive church leader has an ego problem. Jesus says, "Everything they do is done for men to see" (Mt 23:5). For them, looking good is everything. It's not important to *be* people of God, but only to *appear* to be people of God. More impor-

tant than who they are is what people think of them. For this reason
they take for themselves honorific titles such as "Rabbi" (v. 7)—or the
modern equivalent, "Senior Pastor," "Reverend" or "Doctor." True
shepherds need not feign devotion to God, nor do they need exalted
titles. They are known by their fruit.

In chapter six we discover an additional indication of spiritual abusiveness—majoring on minors and neglecting what is truly important.
Spiritually abusive leaders and systems take uncompromising stands
on items of little importance while neglecting issues of significance.
They may possess strong views about styles of dress and wine at
dinner, for instance, but care little about justice and love. True shepherds, however, make love of God and love of people their priority.

In chapter seven we will discuss who gets hooked by spiritual abuse
and why. We look at the emotional needs of the victims as well as the
psychology of the perpetrators.

Chapter eight is devoted to God's cure for spiritual abuse for perpetrators and victims alike. Here we find how the abuser and the
abused are delivered from their mutually destructive relationship
through God's powerful grace.

The last two chapters describe the healthy servant leader. The nonabusive church leader is not weak or passive but strong and full of
authority. Yet this authority arises not from seizing power but from
serving. Nonabusive leaders serve well by lifting burdens off
shoulders, by promoting others, by opening wide the door of the kingdom of God's grace and by feeding nourishing spiritual food to God's
people.

Several of the early reviewers of this book observed that it seems
to be addressed to more than one audience. One pastor said,

At first I thought the audience of the book was those who had been
spiritually abused. As I read it, however, I found myself looking at
the material from different perspectives. At times I was a pastor
learning to counsel someone who had been abused, sometimes I

was a church leader who needed to guard against the attitudes or actions which could lead to abuse. At other times I asked myself if a past event in my church wasn't in fact spiritual abuse.

In fact, the book does speak to a range of audiences, primarily because the Scripture on which it is based is addressed to different audiences. In Matthew 23 Jesus speaks to at least two groups of people—spiritual abusers and their victims. Scripture is often helpful to different groups for different reasons. It is also often helpful to the same person for different reasons. I hope that the same will be true of this book— but I have tried to make it clear which group I am addressing at each point along the way.

Let me say a final word to readers who are victims of spiritual abuse. This book will most likely heighten your awareness of what you suffered and (for a time at least) intensify the pain. If the pain promotes healing, well and good. But if it incites bitterness toward the abuser or an abusive institution, then you will be worse off than before. As angry as Jesus was toward the spiritual abusers of his day, he stood ready to forgive them in an instant. His own power to forgive resides within us, and we are wise to avail ourselves of it.

Jesus said, "In the same way you judge others, you will be judged, and with the measure you use, it will be measured to you" (Mt 7:2). He also said, "All who draw the sword will die by the sword" (Mt 26:52). When someone criticizes his own profession (as I have done in this book), he holds that sword of criticism by its sharp blade so that as he wields it the first blood drawn is his own. I am the pastor of a church and therefore a possible spiritual abuser. In writing this book, I became aware of my own potential to abuse and, I hope, have become less likely to do so. I pray that those who read this book will receive the same benefit.

It is the half-Christian clergy of every denomination that are the cause of the so-called failure of the church.
George MacDonald

Ethics are for dream land. Power is for reality. A leader must have power to control his environment and get things done.
A modern business executive

The teachers of the law and the Pharisees sit in Moses' seat.
Jesus Christ

2

THE SEAT OF MOSES—THE POWER TO ABUSE

*M**y wife, Patti, has given birth* to seven healthy children. One month before she was due to deliver number four, she began to bleed. I rushed her to the hospital for an examination. The diagnosis was placenta previa, a dangerous, sometimes fatal condition in which the placenta attaches too low in the uterus, blocking the birth canal. If Patti had gone into full labor, the placenta blocking the baby's exit would have ruptured. Without immediate medical intervention she would have bled to death, with the baby trapped inside.

A whole and healthy life had formed within Patti. A few years ago (before emergency C-sections were perfected) that life would have died within her because of a small but strategically placed obstruction.

Small but strategically placed obstructions can trap and kill the life of a church too. Most often, these obstructions are defective leaders. A friend of mine says, "In the church everything rises and falls on leadership." For the most part, I agree. My files bulge with examples of strategically placed faulty leadership that has thwarted the spiritual life of the church.

In one church, a youth minister created and led programs that drew many students from two local high schools and a junior college. Most of these young people were soundly converted and grounded in the faith through the youth programs. Several of them were then trained and developed into leaders under the expert pastoral care of the youth minister. All in all, this youth program was the finest outreach ever sponsored by that church. Not only did the church grow numerically through its ministry, but the youth program infused spiritual life into the entire congregation. It was the envy of the whole denomination.

It all ended abruptly when a disturbed teenage girl accused the youth minister of making sexual advances to her. Her father was the church treasurer and chairman of the elders' board. He used his strategic influence to have the youth minister fired without an investigation into the charges against him. This abuse of power killed the church's dynamic youth work, and half of the church's families left.

When denominational officers finally investigated the charges against the youth minister, they were found to be false. In fact, the girl had tried to seduce the minister but had failed. She then had made up the story that resulted in the minister's dismissal. The youth minister was publicly exonerated but was so disillusioned by the experience that he left the ministry and, for now, stays away from church altogether. However, he is doing quite well selling life insurance.

Taking Up Position

One strategically misplaced abusive leader has the power to thwart life in the church just as a misplaced placenta blocks life in a mother's womb. Jesus understood this. In Matthew 23 (as well as in other places) he spoke out strongly against it. In Jesus' day the strategically misplaced leaders were the scribes and the Pharisees. These spiritual leaders worked hard from the beginning to thwart Jesus and the ministry of life that he brought.[1] In a commentary on Matthew 23, Dale Brunner says, "In this chapter Jesus excoriates false religion, especially false religious leadership. Jesus believed that the major problem in Israel was Pharisaism. . . . It was the Pharisaic leadership that diverted Israel from Jesus and so kept Israel from the kingdom of heaven that was breaking in through Jesus."[2]

The Pharisees set themselves up as rulers and judges of the people so as to create a certain type of religious community. A leading characteristic of this community was its preoccupation with purity. The Pharisees were rigid and obsessive about physical and moral cleanness. Jews who conformed to their purity code were considered members of society in good standing. The Pharisees barred from the community those who did not or could not conform. Their power to rule on who was "in" and who was "out" is made clear in John 12:42-43. Here we see that many Jewish leaders believed in Jesus but would not admit it for fear that the Pharisees would excommunicate them from the synagogue. The Pharisees' power to decide who was in and who was outside the community was their power to abuse.

A significant point of conflict between Jesus and the Pharisees was his attack on their purity laws. He went out of his way to break these rules publicly and to teach against them. This had the effect of breaking down the religious-community boundaries which the Pharisees had so carefully constructed. They wanted to be the gatekeepers, controlling who was accepted and who was rejected. But Jesus let everyone, even prostitutes and tax collectors, into his new community—a fellowship that was outside the Pharisees' control. No wonder they hated him.

Today, when church leaders set themselves up as keepers of the gate, using religious performance rather than faith in Jesus as the criterion for acceptance or rejection, they become the strategically misplaced leaders who thwart the life of the body of Christ. In so doing, they perpetuate the ministry of the Pharisees.

In most cases of spiritual abuse, the control of people is the central issue. As Jesus proclaimed God's new community, setting himself up as its leader, the Pharisees saw their control over society slipping away. This not only incited their wrath against the Lord but galvanized them to wield their power against him. Abuse requires power, and the Pharisees had it.

Religious scrupulosity and a desire to control others made the Pharisees the most dangerous of men. As C. S. Lewis once said, "If the divine call does not make us better, it will make us very much worse. Of all bad men, religious bad men are the worst."[3]

Jesus was often curt with the Pharisees, but on the occasion recorded in Matthew 23 he lets his anger burn white-hot against them. If a person is characteristically impatient and given to outbursts of rage, his anger is neither impressive nor effective. But if a person is usually gentle and patient, and then explodes into blazing wrath, it shocks us. This is why Jesus' anger toward Israel's spiritual leadership in Matthew 23 is so arresting.

Our anger begets various consequences. One of the most interesting of these is the revelation of our true commitments. We only get angry about the issues we care about. I am angered at the long lines I get stuck in while waiting for service. This shows that I care about being inconvenienced. When my three older sons do not clean up the garage after woodworking, I am angered; this shows my commitment to a clean garage. And if, like Jesus, we get angry at spiritual abusers, it may indicate our deep concern for their victims. As David Seamands explains, "A person who cannot feel anger at evil is a person who lacks enthusiasm for good. If you cannot hate the wrong, it is very questionable whether you really love righteousness."[4]

The New Testament records several accounts of Jesus' anger that reveal what he really cares about. We discover in each of these events that Jesus cares about people above religion. His deep concern for people who are victimized by false religious authority comes through clearly in Matthew 23. One of the benefits of seeing Jesus' anger against the Pharisees here is that it provides today's victims of spiritual abuse the permission they may need to break free from their abusers.

Jesus begins his exposé of the Pharisees by showing us how they had seized the power with which they controlled their followers. Their power base was the seat of Moses. He said, "The teachers of the law and the Pharisees sit in Moses' seat" (Mt 23:2). Moses' seat was not a mere metaphor; it was an actual stone chair or throne placed in front of a synagogue.[5] The Pharisee ascended this seat of authority to assume spiritual power over the common people. The Pharisees took this position of power for themselves. They were neither appointed by God nor elected by the people. They sat themselves down in Moses' seat and grabbed for themselves the authority to rule.[6]

We often hear today that "knowledge is power." In Jesus' day, the knowledge of the law of Moses was power. The Pharisees knew Moses' teaching by heart and knew how to teach and apply it. They were the experts. From this lofty position of power they looked down on the "mob" (as they called them), which they said was cursed because "it knows nothing of the law" (Jn 7:49). So for these ecclesiastical abusers of the first century, the seat of Moses functioned in much the same way as leadership titles, academic degrees and church offices do for today's spiritual abusers.

Authority Props

I have heard pastors say to their congregations, "Because I am the pastor, you must follow me." Their demand was not based on the truth or the God-directedness of their leadership but on their title. That is a false basis of authority. I've heard other religious leaders say, in effect, "Because I have a Ph.D., you have to take my words seriously." If their words are not true, they have no authority and we need not listen to them; their degrees are irrelevant. The ultimate appeal to position is the Roman pope's claim to infallibility based on his being successor to St. Peter. (This is especially interesting since Peter is the only person Jesus ever referred to as "Satan"; he is also the disciple who denied Jesus three times. Peter also proved to be quite fallible in his controversy with Paul; see Galatians 2.)

Any appeal to authority based on position, title, degree or office is false. The only authority God recognizes and to which we should submit is the truth.

Men (and sometimes women) who take for themselves "seats of authority" often feel the need to embellish their offices, positions or titles with additional "special claims." They may point to their "unique calling," their "singular abilities," their "great experience" or their "prophetic revelation" to back up their office or their position. None of these special claims necessarily has anything to do with true spiritual authority.

Another trick used to keep leaders firmly perched on Moses' chair and above accountability is to refer to them as "the Lord's anointed." This supposedly means that they have been especially chosen and gifted by God and so should be treated with special reverence. The Old Testament command "Touch not the Lord's anointed" is employed to protect these leaders from examination or criticism. This phrase, which comes from 1 Chronicles 16:22 and Psalm 105:15, is taken out of context and twisted to meet the need. When David uttered these words he was warning his men not to kill King Saul, whom the Lord himself had anointed with oil and the Holy Spirit.

David's warning not to kill the king has nothing whatever to do with our treatment of church leaders today. Ancient Israel's class system, with its hierarchy of kings, prophets and priests, is abolished in the New Testament. We have one King, and the rest of us are priests who are all exhorted to prophesy. The exclusive spiritual anointing that came upon the kings, prophets and priests in the Old Testament is now lavishly poured out on all God's people. To speak of anyone as especially anointed like the Old Testament leaders encourages an exaggerated awe of that person. It also implies a class system in the kingdom of God, where no such system exists.

If by appealing to position, unique claims or special anointings, leaders succeed in creating a hierarchy in the church, they can more easily control those beneath them. They can also defend themselves against any who might challenge them.

Watchman Nee may have unwittingly aided many of today's church leaders in creating just such a structure. Nee wrote that if you truly understand Jesus as the head of the body, you will also see that other members of the body are above you in rank and that you must submit to them. "Hence you recognize not only the head but also those whom God has set in his body to represent the head. If you are at odds with them, you will be at odds with God."[7] Nee states elsewhere that we are expected to blindly obey those in delegated authority over us and that "insubordination is rebellion and for this the one under authority must answer to God."[8]

Some opportunistic church leaders have built upon Nee's error, saying that Jesus now "rules through delegated authority—i.e., those whom he sets in authority under himself. Wherever his delegated authority touches our lives, he requires us to acknowledge and submit to it, just as we would to him in person."[9] Another misguided leader puts it this way:

A disciple is one who obeys his disciplers even if he doesn't comprehend what he's told. Because he wants to have a teachable heart he will fully obey and be totally obedient even if what he's asked to do is contrary to what he would normally do or think. To distrust the person God had put in his life is equal to distrusting God and his faith in God is shown by his faith in his disciples.[10]

Paul knew otherwise and demonstrated it as he confronted his senior, the apostle Peter, as recounted in Galatians 2. When Paul discovered that Peter was "not acting in line with the truth of the gospel" (v. 14), he "opposed him to his face, because he was in the wrong" (v. 11).

Among other things, Paul declared by this action that the truth always outranks position or title in the church. Truth and its authority are not rooted in a personality or office. It is derived from the Word of God and the gospel it proclaims. I concur with Michael Horton, who maintains that "there is no such thing as 'The Lord's Anointed,' preachers who are above the Word. . . . Any claim to divine authority for commands, expectations, revelations, or guidance that are not stated in the pages of Holy Scripture are marks of a spiritual tyrant and Pharisee."[11]

Ignoring this most obvious of New Testament teachings, many leaders today have fashioned for themselves ecclesiastical hierarchies with themselves at the top. Out of this twisted image of the body of Christ comes the supporting idea of "spiritual covering," which functions as yet another tool of control. Spiritual covering pictures a chain of command with authority flowing through the chain from top to bottom. Those lower on the chain are to see those above them as their "covering" and submit to them as they would to Christ himself.

Most false doctrines result from overemphasizing a biblical truth, thus making it an untruth, or taking a biblical truth out of context and twisting it to a purpose the Holy Spirit did not intend. The notion of spiritual covering is a different kind of false doctrine. Not only is there little or no biblical basis for the idea of covering, but it flies in the face of numerous broad-based, biblical teachings to the contrary: the egalitarian nature of church fellowship (Mt 23:8-12), the fraternal nature of church discipline (Mt 18) and the parity among members of the body of Christ (1 Cor 12:14-26). In Matthew 10:1 Jesus gave his disciples spiritual authority and the power to heal the sick and cast out demons. While Jesus delegated to his followers his authority over sickness and evil spirits, he never delegated his authority over people to anyone.

Some church leaders defend their heavy-handed, autocratic style of leadership and their hierarchical church structure in the name of "church unity." Only a strong central authority, they imply, can maintain discipline and "unity among the brethren." The problem, of course, is that real unity can never be achieved by coercion. Christian authoritarianism confuses spiritual unity with unanimity. Unity is achieved as free people freely submit to one another. How it happens is a mystery; the process is often very messy and requires mutual risk-taking. Unanimity or uniformity, on the other hand, can be achieved with autocratic controls. It can be prescribed, measured and moni-tored. It is essentially external, whereas true unity is first internal. Uniformity looks for correct behavior, whereas unity wants a right spirit. Unanimity demands that we all experience God in the same ways and express that experience with the same vocabulary. Unity delights in differences.

Spiritual abusers are able to impose unanimity and uniformity be-cause of the authoritarian hierarchies they construct. This is also how they are able to demand preferential treatment and honor.

The honor we give our leaders, however, can only be offered freely. It is not based on a seat of authority, but on leadership that is an expression of servanthood. Our true leaders are servants of Christ and of us.

Servant Leadership

Jesus stated clearly that the only legitimate spiritual authority is servant authority. He said that although rulers in the world's business and government lord it over their followers, "not so with you." If anyone wishes to be great, that is well and good, but great-ness should be expressed through servanthood. The one with true

authority will serve as a slave, not as a ruler (Mt 20:24-28; see also Jn
13). This one insight makes the true authorities in the church easy
to discern.

In Luke 12:42 Jesus gives a picture of true spiritual authority in
the form of a parable. He asks, "Who then is the faithful and wise
manager, whom the master puts in charge of his servants to give them
their food allowance at the proper time?" True leaders are not necessarily profoundly gifted or conspicuously talented; they need no exalted office; they need no titles to validate their words; they need no
seat of Moses to support their effectiveness. All they need to do is be
faithful and wise, serving food to their followers as it is needed.

I am acquainted with pastors and church leaders who feel the need
of titles and special recognition in order to gain the respect of their
followers. They attempt to appear decisive and forceful to win their
people's confidence, but all Jesus expects of them is to cook nourishing (not necessarily fancy) spiritual food and know when to serve it.
When Jesus compares a good leader to a faithful and wise household
cook, he does not offer this definition as one option among many. In
the kingdom of God, servant leadership is the only kind of leadership
there is. If a minister rejects it, judgment is swift and severe. The
abusive leader will receive a beating (vv. 47-48) and may even be "cut
. . . to pieces" (v. 46).

Jesus not only instructed leaders to serve in the manner of a household servant, but he *showed* us how to do it. In his culture, the task
of washing the feet of the guests as they entered a home fell to the
lowest-ranked servant. As Jesus washed the feet of his followers, he
said to them, "You call me 'Teacher' and 'Lord,' and rightly so, for that
is what I am. Now that I, your Lord and Teacher, have washed your
feet, you also should wash one another's feet. I have set you an example" (Jn 13:13-15). In Jesus' church, true spiritual authority does
not ascend the seat of Moses to rule but kneels down to serve.

Jesus' servant leadership was not merely a mode of self-revelation, a temporary expression of his larger work among us. "Servant" is who Jesus is—yesterday, today and forever. Jesus once told a parable about his Second Coming and said, "It will be good for those servants whose master finds them watching when he comes." And then he shocked those who expected him to return as the sword-wielding judge. He said, to the contrary, that "he will dress himself to serve, will have [his servants] recline at the table and will come and wait on them" (Lk 12:35-40).

Paul sees clearly that Jesus' style of servant leadership is ours as well. Our attitude, he says, "should be the same as that of Christ Jesus: Who, being in very nature God, did not consider equality with God something to be grasped, but made himself nothing, taking on the very nature of a servant" (Phil 2:5-7). Jesus laid aside his positional authority as God and took up his functional authority as a servant. As his followers, we may not reject servant authority to take over the seat of positional authority.

Positional authority carries with it the power to coerce, to compel. Servant authority, however, cheerfully forfeits this power, so that those who submit to it can only do so freely and voluntarily.

To begin with, Jesus calls us to follow him but does not coerce us. He leads without forcing us to follow. During his years of ministry on earth, would-be disciples who decided not to pay the price of following him were sent away. Jesus leads through friendship rather than fear. His sovereign grace enables us to submit to his lordship (which is the best decision of our lives), but it does not determine that decision. Once we are born into a saving relationship with him, he continues to uphold our freedom to chose. Every day of our lives he invites us to voluntarily follow him. At no point does he employ his all-encompassing authority to compel us to follow.

The apostle Paul seemed to have thoroughly integrated Jesus' non-coercive, nonabusive style of leadership into his own ministry. First of all, he taught that the body of Christ is a nonhierarchical living organism. He explained that God himself is so committed to absolute parity among the members of the body that he actually makes adjustments to give greater honor to those members who otherwise lack it (1 Cor 12:24-25).

Though Paul recognized the offices of apostle, prophet, evangelist and the like, he understood these to be gifts or resources for the body. There is no hint in Paul's writing that these offices constitute a pyramidal power structure. When Paul's own converts rejected his leadership, he did not pull rank to force them back into line. Although Paul was the most apostolic-minded of all the apostles, he used no official or ecclesiastical power to defend his authority. When confronting rivals and detractors in Corinth, he says, "By the meekness and gentleness of Christ, I appeal to you" (2 Cor 10:1; see also Rom 10:1; 2 Cor 1:24; 8:8; 1 Thess 2:7; Philem 8-9).

Paul never appealed to the seat of Moses or its equivalent to get his way. Instead he made himself vulnerable to his followers, inviting them to respond in kind: "We have spoken freely to you, Corinthians, and opened wide our hearts to you. We are not withholding our affection from you, but you are withholding yours from us. As a fair exchange—I speak as to my children—open wide your hearts also" (2 Cor 6:11-13).

We have looked at how true authority arises out of service and is submitted to voluntarily. Defining leadership and followership in these terms makes spiritual abuse virtually impossible.

Following or Resisting

But someone might say, "What about 1 Thessalonians 5:12-13?" There Paul says, "Now we ask you, brothers, to respect those who work hard among you, who are over you in the Lord and who admonish you. Hold them in the highest regard in love because of their work. Live in peace with each other."

These leaders whom Paul exhorts us to hold in "highest regard" have earned that regard only because they "work hard" among us and for us.

Someone else might say, "What about Hebrews 13:17?" Here the writer tells us, "Obey your leaders and submit to their authority. They keep watch over you as men who must give an account." To begin with, this verse does not apply to any leader who does not function first of all as a servant "watching over" the followers. Second, the New Testament word here for "obey" *(peithomai)* does not refer to the obedience that may be demanded by right or imposed by decree. Rather, this kind of trust is given voluntarily to leaders in response to their character and the power of their persuasion.[12] Commenting on Hebrews 13:17, Ray Peacock says, "Such obedience does not demolish the will of an individual demanding blind adherence to whatever is commanded, but invites that person to consider thoughtfully, allowing his conscience to be the final arbiter before God."[13]

Robert Clinton follows this line in his comments on spiritual authority. "Persuasive power," he says, "gains compliance of the follower yet protects the freedom of the follower to exercise moral responsibility."[14]

The New Testament makes clear to spiritual leaders that they have no official or ecclesiastical power by which to lead. They may only appeal to their followers and persuade them to cooperate. By reading the New Testament, followers should understand that they cannot be coerced or shamed into submitting to any leader. They are free to cooperate or not.

Why is it then that those who sit themselves down in Moses' seat (then and now) are so effective at controlling, manipulating and abusing God's people? I will discuss the psychology of the abuser and the abused in subsequent chapters. For now, let me make some basic observations about why otherwise sensible and intelligent people submit to spiritual abuse.

In every known human society it appears that most people wish to be led. They follow the line of least resistance, letting those in positions of power make decisions for them. The Bible seems to recognize this, referring to us most often as "sheep." This means that we have the tendency to let authority figures make the rules and then apply them to us. When they administer the rules in an abusive manner, we will (at first) tend to submit.

Combined with our tendency to want a leader is our incurably religious nature. Our longing for God is essential to us. It is the most significant aspect of our being. Those who sit themselves down in Moses' seat and pose as mediators for God can therefore play on our desire for a leader *and* our yearning for God. It is no surprise then that those who most earnestly desire to please God are most apt to be victimized by spiritual authorities setting themselves up as mediators for God. The spiritually keen are most at risk.

Over the years I have seen many Christian wives wrongly submit to violently abusive husbands because of their intense (although misguided) desire to submit to God's authority. Others have conscientiously stayed in abusive churches for the same wrong reasons.

It should be comforting to realize that the hurt you may have suffered from church leaders in the past could be due not to something wrong about you but something *right:* your longing to get close to God and to please him.

Nevertheless, Christ calls us to spiritual maturity. And that sometimes means resisting spiritual authorities just as he did. I agree with Stephen Arterburn and Jack Felton, who say, "We must have the courage to follow Christ's example and overturn the system, be it a marriage or an organization, if that system is wrong. Silent submission in the face of violence, dishonesty and abuse will only enable that abuse to be passed on to generations."[15]

We will always want leaders and we will always need God, so we must learn to distinguish the good leaders from the abusive ones. In the next chapter we will consider how to do just that.

We must not think the worst of good truths for their being preached by bad ministers; nor good laws for their being enforced by bad magistrates.
Matthew Henry

Be careful. . . . Be on your guard against the yeast of the Pharisees and Sadducees.
Jesus Christ

3

SNIFFING OUT THE
YEAST OF THE
PHARISEES

*T*he Pharisees were the official, ordained Bible teachers of their community. They seemed highly qualified to teach the Scripture because of their great learning. They memorized vast portions of the Bible (even entire books). They were also well schooled in applying Scripture. If the common folk wanted to know the text that applied to a particular life situation, a Pharisee could tell them. These Bible scholars were hard-working, disciplined and, in the popular mind, very moral.

They were the most respected men of their community, yet Jesus intensely disliked them—or at least he acted as if he did. He called them names, denounced their actions and rejected their teachings. Whenever he referred to them in his own teaching, he used them as negative examples. Though they knew the words of the Bible, Jesus said, they missed its message. Speaking directly to them, Jesus said, "And the Father who sent me has himself testified concerning me. You have never heard his voice nor seen his form, nor does his word dwell in you, for you do not believe the one he sent. You diligently study the Scriptures because you think that by them you possess eternal life. These are the Scriptures that testify about me, yet you refuse to come to me to have life" (Jn 5:37-40).

Missing Jesus and therefore missing life was their own loss. But what upset Jesus more was how they denied life to the common people, the ones who looked to them for leadership. Matthew 9:35-36 implies clearly that in Jesus' mind, those posing as shepherds for the people of Israel were useless and even harmful: "Jesus went through all the towns and villages, teaching in their synagogues, preaching the good news of the kingdom and healing every disease and sickness. When he saw the crowds, he had compassion on them, because they were harassed and helpless, like sheep without a shepherd."

It seems that when Jesus stood up in the synagogues, with many Pharisees and others present, he stated that the crowds were harassed and helpless like sheep without a shepherd. This constituted one of the most provocative challenges imaginable. Picture yourself standing up next Sunday in a large church service with many of the pastoral staff present. Then hear yourself saying, "This congregation is distressed, anxious and powerless because you have no real pastors!"

Using the Sheep

Jesus examined the Pharisees' performance and found it wanting. As he did so, he surely had in mind the shepherds of Ezekiel's day. The job description of the shepherds in ancient Israel is most clearly spelled out in Ezekiel 34 (though it is stated in negative terms). In this chapter God calls his pastors in for a performance review and flunks them.

Woe to the shepherds of Israel who only take care of themselves!

Should not shepherds take care of the flock? You eat the curds, clothe yourselves with the wool and slaughter the choice animals, but you do not take care of the flock. You have not strengthened the weak or healed the sick or bound up the injured. You have not brought back the strays or searched for the lost. You have ruled them harshly and brutally. So they were scattered because there was no shepherd, and when they were scattered they became food for all the wild animals. (vv. 2-5)

Pastors in the Western world are most often judged on their preaching and administrative skills, but when God reviewed his pastors he did not mention these criteria. He indicted the leaders of Israel for not strengthening the weak or healing the sick. They had not "brought back the strays or searched for the lost." That is to say, they had found something more important to do than caring for the people, which was their real job. Furthermore, they ruled the flock harshly (v. 4), or, as Jesus would say later, "They tie up heavy loads and put them on men's shoulders, but they themselves are not willing to lift a finger to move them" (Mt 23:4).

Both Ezekiel and Jesus condemned one fundamental error in the shepherds: they used the sheep rather than served them. They acted as if the sheep existed to meet their needs rather than the other way around. When shepherds today look out over their congregations and see their people as church growth statistics, tithing units and workers in their programs, they follow the pastoral style that Jesus and Ezekiel prophesied against.

Traditions of the Elders

In general, Jesus saw the shepherds of his day as equally useless and harmful as the shepherds of Ezekiel's day. In Matthew 15:1-14 Jesus makes clear that the Pharisees' teaching and practices are not to be followed. The action here begins with the Pharisees rebuking Jesus for letting his followers "break the tradition of the elders"—that is, they did not wash their hands before eating (v. 2). Jesus responds by asking them bluntly, "And why do you break the command of God?" (v. 3). In the verses that follow, he shows us how many of those who pose as Bible defenders are actually Bible breakers. They wash their hands, all right, but they abuse the parents whom God commanded them to honor (vv. 3-6).

Jesus refers to these so-called Bible defenders as "hypocrites" and quotes Isaiah to say that "their teachings are but rules taught by men" (v. 8). It may be surprising to realize that these "rules taught by men," or as the Pharisees put it, "the traditions of the elders," were the first Bible commentaries. These "traditions of the elders" were the authoritative interpretations and applications of the Hebrew Scriptures. Our modern equivalent would be our most respected interpretations and applications of the Christian faith.

Depending on your background, the traditions of *your* elders might include *The Works of St. Augustine,* Calvin's *Institutes of the Christian Religion, The Works of Luther, The Westminster Confession* or Karl Barth's *Church Dogmatics.* As valuable as these traditions may be, Jesus implied that the Scriptures themselves are primary. This means that leaders especially must make Bible study a priority. Putting Scripture at the center does not absolutely ensure against abuse, but focusing on the traditions of human beings makes abuse more likely.

Jesus concludes his warning against the Pharisees' teaching in Matthew 15 by saying, "Leave them; they are blind guides. If a blind man leads a blind man, both will fall into a pit" (v. 14).

Beware of the Yeast

Jesus continues warning his disciples about the Pharisees in Matthew 16:6-12:

"Be careful," Jesus said to them. "Be on your guard against the yeast of the Pharisees and Sadducees."

They discussed this among themselves and said, "It is because we didn't bring any bread."

Aware of their discussion, Jesus asked, "You of little faith, why are you talking among yourselves about having no bread? Do you still not understand? Don't you remember the five loaves for the five thousand, and how many basketfuls you gathered? Or the seven loaves for the four thousand, and how many basketfuls you gathered? How is it you don't understand that I was not talking to you about bread? But be on your guard against the yeast of the Pharisees and Sadducees." Then they understood that he was not telling them to guard against the yeast used in bread, but against the teaching of the Pharisees and Sadducees.

Jesus begins by warning, "Be careful. . . . Be on your guard against the yeast of the Pharisees and Sadducees" (v. 6). The disciples are momentarily confused, thinking that he is speaking of actual bread yeast. But for the Jews, yeast was a metaphor for evil. Yeast mixed into a lump of dough works invisibly and silently to transform its nature, slowly but surely. Just so, Jesus is saying, theological yeast mixed into a body of biblical truth gradually but inevitably transforms and destroys that truth.

Yeast is the irresistible power of corruption. It is the putrefaction of evil that permeates truth, changing it into a mixture of truth and lie. This is, of course, far more dangerous than a pure lie, because that is easily spotted and rejected. Lie hidden within truth tricks us into acceptance.

Jesus did not warn his disciples to beware of the yeast of the prostitutes and the tax collectors—the "lowlifes" of his day. Their evil is obvious, of course, and therefore relatively harmless. The true danger is the high-sounding religious lie mixed into a body of truth spoken by a person of respect. Jesus warns us to be on guard against those who present themselves as religious authorities. As Philip Keller says in his book *Predators in Our Pulpits,* "The greatest threat to the church today is not from without but from our own leadership within."[1]

What then was the theological yeast that Jesus warned his disciples of? And in what guises does it come to us today? According to Dale Brunner's commentary on this passage, the yeast of the Pharisees is their "perfectionist theology"[2]—that is, the idea that performing religious duties gains us a higher standing with God and secures his blessings. Or as William Hendriksen says, the yeast of the Pharisees and Sadducees was "the basic principle which governed their lives as shown in their effort to attain 'salvation' or 'security' by their own efforts. Religion . . . was outward conformity to a certain standard."[3]

The modern equivalent of the "yeast of the Pharisees" is what we call legalism. The term *legalism* covers any variation on the notion that if we do the proper Christian disciplines well enough and long enough, God will be pleased with us and will reward us. It is the idea that if we do more and try harder, we can make a claim on God's favor so that we need not rely totally upon his mercy and grace.

Legalism is the great weapon of spiritual abuse. Multiplying religious rules to gain control over followers is authoritarianism's primary tool. Legalism is an expression of leaders' compulsion to seek security and predictability. If they can enforce an exhaustive list of dos and don'ts, they think, they will gain that security and predictability they crave.

Followers cooperate with this abusive regime because they are told that it is the way to please God and gain his favor. Tragically, this kind of conscientious rule-keeping actually takes us away from God. Any religious activity that implies that Jesus' cross is not enough for our acceptance with God leads us *away from him,* not to him.

The Yeasty Galatians
The apostle Paul picks up yeast as a metaphor for legalism in his

letter to the Galatians. "A little yeast," he warns, "works through the whole batch of dough" (Gal 5:9; see also 1 Cor 5:6-7). For Paul, this "little yeast" is Jewish circumcision and other religious legalisms. Apparently some Christian teachers had followed Paul into Galatia, adding various religious requirements to his gospel of salvation through faith in Christ alone. These so-called Judaizers did not deny salvation through faith in Christ. They simply added to it a few Jewish disciplines, supposedly to help the Gentile believers go on to maturity (Gal 3:3). They said, in effect, "Jesus gets us started in the Christian life, but we become mature through our own religious performance."

Modern evangelicals are much like the Galatians when we let ourselves be loaded down with works of the law in hopes that through them we may attain our goal. We so easily believe the lie that if we try harder and do more, maturity, holiness and blessedness will necessarily result.

Words about "acceptance through grace alone and the cross alone" are, of course, present in today's legalistic teaching. Gospel words cover the lie of legalism so that we swallow a toxic mixture of truth and error. The result is spiritual sickness.

I recently attended two conferences on consecutive weekends at a local church. The theme of the first was "grace," while the second had to do with "holiness." The speakers at the first conference taught the standard Reformation truths of "salvation by grace alone," "salvation by faith alone" and "sanctification by keeping in step with the Spirit."

But the teachers at the "holiness conference" on the following weekend contradicted virtually all of this teaching. They taught that while God accepts us initially through the cross of Christ, we must "work to show ourselves approved for his higher purposes." They made it clear that God ranks and promotes his followers according to their relative holiness (and holiness was defined in cultural rather than New Testament terms). They repeatedly stated that "God will

not entrust his power and authority to unclean vessels." This conference aimed to enlist those who attended into God's "Holy End-Times
Army," which would usher in the return of Christ.

Such "holiness" and "revival" teachings are among the dreary, joyless heresies periodically afflicting the church, much as the annual flu
plague afflicts the general population. This congregation should have
spotted the yeasty character of legalism, especially in view of the
foundational teaching on grace that they received the week prior. But
because the "holiness" teaching was billed as a "balance" to the grace
message (as if error could balance truth), it was accepted. This mixture of truth and lie was damaging for many; for some the consequences may have been spiritually lethal.

According to Paul, spiritual yeast actually may cause spiritual
death. He says quite bluntly that basing our relationship with God on
Christ's work *and* our own efforts actually destroys that relationship,
making it of "no value" (Gal 5:2). The yeast of the Pharisees poisons
the bread of life.

In Paul's view, a Gentile who enters into Christ through faith and
then lets himself be circumcised in order to add to Christ's work ends
up losing Christ. Such people are "alienated from Christ" and "fallen
away from grace" (Gal 5:4). He maintains that the small cut of circumcision is nothing short of life-threatening. We see a similar metaphor in 2 Timothy 2:17, where the yeast of false teaching is likened
to gangrene; left untreated, it will destroy the entire organism.

Martin Luther, in his commentary on Galatians, says that to add
any religious work to the gospel of grace seems to be a trivial matter,
but "it does more damage than human reason can imagine. Not only
does it mar and obscure the knowledge of grace but it also removes
Christ and all of his blessings and it completely overthrows the gospel."[4]

Paul is frustrated and angry that the Galatians are destroying the
gospel of Christ by letting religious law be added to it. Reminding

them of their start in the Christian life, he says, "You foolish Galatians! Who has bewitched you? Before your very eyes Jesus Christ was clearly portrayed as crucified" (3:1). He then says, in effect, that mature Christian life is not a mixture of grace and law but grace alone. "Are you so foolish? After beginning with the Spirit, are you now trying to attain your goal by human effort?" (3:3).

Just like Jesus, Paul reserves his most hostile language for religious teachers who knead the yeast of human performance into God's acceptance by grace. Calling the Galatians "bewitched" suggests that their false teachers are witches. "Bewitched" refers to "the evil eye," which was the primary mode of witchcraft in the Mediterranean world.[5] The evil eye was a witch's spell that slowly sucked the life out of its victim (an apt description of legalism). Anyone who rejected life as God's gift and returned to working for it would surely lose that life. In Paul's thinking, anyone who acted in such a foolish, self-destructive way must certainly be bewitched.

It is vital to remember that those who cast these life-sucking theological spells did not look like witches, even though they were. They looked instead like Pharisees: respected, highly disciplined and godly. Luther comments, "The holier the heretics seem to be, the more dangerous their cause. If the false apostles had not possessed outstanding gifts, great authority, and the appearance of holiness; and if they had not claimed to be ministers of Christ and sincere preachers of the gospel . . . they could not have so easily made an impression on the Galatians."[6]

Paul's discernment of these false teachers is not based on their appearance, their gifts, their eloquence, their learning or their experience. In brief, he does not hold these impressive leaders in the same esteem the Galatians do. Paul does not care how talented they are or how godly they appear. He wants to know whether they remain faithful to the gospel of grace. Seeing that they do not, he calls them witches and demands absolute intolerance of them. For Paul, adding any Pharisaical works to the finished work of Christ is not just off-center; it is evil and must be rejected (Gal 5:7-12).

A Seeming Contradiction

In the same way, when Jesus tells us to beware of the yeast of the Pharisees, he means we should hold ourselves back from their legalism (Mt 16:6). Religious rules look and sound godly but are, in fact, spiritual poison. Self-effort holiness is not a more sincere expression of faith; it is witchcraft and the destruction of faith.

If we must reject the yeasty, legalistic teaching of the Pharisees, what then are we to make of Jesus' words in Matthew 23:3: "So you must obey [the Pharisees] and do everything they tell you. But do not do what they do, for they do not practice what they preach"? How do we square "Be on your guard against the yeast of the Pharisees" (Mt 16:6) with "You must obey them"?

Most commentators solve the contradiction in Matthew 23:3 in much the same way as R. V. G. Tasker does: "Jesus recognizes the rightful claims of the scribes, the legal experts of the Pharisaical party, to be exponents of the law; and so long as they confine themselves to that task, their words, he insists, are to be respected, even if the conduct of some of them is inconsistent with their teaching."[7]

That is to say, so long as these teachers teach Scripture and apply it rightly, we are to follow what they say—but we are to do so with a critical eye and a discerning heart. The human tendency is to accept or reject a body of teaching whole. In general, if a teaching seems good, it is swallowed completely and uncritically. When elements in that teaching later prove to be erroneous and hurtful, the entire body of it is often rejected.

In my own congregation there are people who in the past sat under the teaching of the "health and wealth gospel" preachers. These preachers said that if people sent their money to the ministry, it would be returned to them tenfold. When that didn't happen, the people became embittered and rejected the true biblical teaching on tithing and giving to God's work.

When abusive preachers base their erroneous teaching on the Bible and then their ministry proves to be defective, some will throw the Bible teaching out with the yeast that was mixed into it. This is why Matthew Henry says that "we must not think the worst of good truths for their being preached by bad ministers; nor good laws for their being enforced by bad magistrates."[8]

Taken in context, Jesus' endorsement of the teaching of the Pharisees in Matthew 23 seems to be a qualification of the withering attack that follows. Despite Jesus' apparent utter rejection of the Pharisees in Matthew 23, he does not want any valid biblical teaching to be lost. Jesus wants us to respect church officeholders and to give them a fair hearing.

The Bereans can be our example, for they gave Paul a full and fair hearing which was at the same time critical. According to Luke, "the Bereans were of more noble character than the Thessalonians, for they received the message with great eagerness and examined the Scriptures every day to see if what Paul said was true" (Acts 17:11). Like the Jews of Berea, we are to discern carefully what we are taught.

Jesus' teaching in Matthew 23:1-3 calls us to maturity and the right kind of independence from religious authority. From this point he goes on to expose abusive religious authorities and their practices. Jesus finally calls us to reject these abusers and to overthrow their religious systems.

There is no way to disarm any man except through guilt.... If there is not enough guilt, we must create it.... But save us from the man of clear conscience.
Ayn Rand

Jesus said, "You shall know the truth and the truth will set you free." If that's true then much of the church doesn't know the truth, since it is often a place of bondage.
A South African missionary

They tie up heavy loads and put them on men's shoulders.
Jesus Christ

4
HEAVY
LOADS

*A**lice is a sixty-five-year-old wid-*
ow. Her husband died last year of lung cancer. When he first became
sick, she turned to religion for comfort and direction. Because she was
at home most of the time to care for her husband, she got her religion
from television. One of her favorite TV evangelists teaches that if
Christians have enough faith, their prayers will get answered; when
they are not answered, it is due to a lack of faith. Alice began to pray
for her husband to be healed, but she had occasional doubts that he
would be. When he died, she assumed it was because of those doubts
that her prayers had failed.

After her husband's funeral, Alice fell into a guilt-induced depression. As a result, she continued to stay at home and became even more
dependent on her TV preachers. The preacher who had promised

answered prayer in exchange for faith also promised abundant life in exchange for religious performance. According to this preacher, God's formula for awarding joy and peace is fasting and prayer—and regular, generous and cheerful giving to God's work.

Alice was eager to atone for the guilt she felt over her husband's death, so she dutifully followed the preacher's formula. She fasted, prayed and wrote checks to his TV ministry. This behavior did not yield the promised peace, so she phoned the ministry to get counsel and prayer. The person she spoke to assured her that "God's word would not return to him void" and "she would in time reap what she had sown." The only advice the telephone counselor had was for her to increase her prayer and her giving; this she did.

Now, months later, she is just as miserable as when she first took up her religious burdens. Only she is out of money and becoming hopeless.

The Yoke of the Law

The abusive spiritual leaders of Jesus' day loaded the common people down with multiple religious rules and regulations. In addition to God's law, they laid on them various layers of human traditions. When the people failed to carry this load, they felt guilty and spiritually defective.

The Pharisees themselves spent many of their waking hours memorizing and discussing God's law and the thousands of man-made refinements surrounding it. They referred to this discipline as "coming under the yoke of the law." Those who mastered this yoke had occasion to boast, but for the common person, who had neither the time nor the means for such mastery, the yoke became an oppressive burden.

Universally, the dominant trait of oppressive religious and governmental systems is the multiplication of rules and regulations. These serve to control behavior when kept and promote guilt when broken.

In either case, the proliferation of law gives authorities control over the people.

Ayn Rand demonstrates the logic of creating laws for guilt manipulation by having one of Utopia's elite say, "There is no way to rule innocent men. The only power any government has is the power to crack down on criminals. . . . So, who wants a nation of law-abiding citizens? What's there in that for anyone? But just pass the kind of laws that can neither be observed nor enforced nor objectively interpreted and you create a nation of law-breakers—and then you cash in on guilt."[1]

"Christian legalism" functions in just this way. Most (but not all) of the so-called holiness and revival preaching I have heard over the years is little other than manipulation to produce guilt. This brand of legalism sets up impossible standards of spiritual purity and performance; if taken seriously, these standards prove that we don't measure up, so we must try harder and do more. Overcome with guilt feelings, we do almost anything to atone for them. When called forward to repent, we go. When commanded to have a longer quiet time, we do (for a little while at least). When money is demanded, we give. As guilt feelings set in (because we have failed to measure up), spiritual abusers can have their way with us.

David Chilton explains some of the consequences of this type of guilt manipulation: "Guilt is an extremely powerful force; when we feel it, we become distracted, confused and incompetent. . . . We become overly dependent on others to make decisions for us, and we begin to avoid necessary confrontations and independent actions. We become slaves."[2]

Alex recently wrote me a twenty-page letter detailing his last three years in the service of an evangelistic mission in the Midwest. From the time he entered the mission, he was told that "Jesus expected total dedication of him," "true disciples must chose between God and comfort," and "sacrifice and dying to self are essential for spiritual growth." All of this, of course, has a ring of truth. But in the hands of religious abusers, the call to radical discipleship becomes a license to control and manipulate.

Alex explained to me how the mission leaders assigned him one degrading job after another, for the purpose (they said) of refining his spirit. One of his tasks was to go out on the road, at his own expense, to raise funds for the mission. When he objected, the leaders told him that he was showing signs of rebellion and that he had a long way to go in "dying to self." Feeling guilty for once again failing to measure up spiritually, he submitted all the more to the heavy loads of the mission leaders.

Guilt Manipulation

Rob and Bev were only seventeen years old when they got married. They wedded young because Bev was pregnant. Both sets of parents supported their marriage but felt shamed by it too. They expressed their disappointment with rebuke: "How could you treat us like this? After all, we trusted you." Bev and Rob worked hard to succeed in their marriage, partly (they admitted) to make it up to their disappointed parents.

In their early twenties, Rob and Bev joined a family-oriented fundamentalist church. They quickly caught the attention of the pastor, who, over time, offered them leadership roles in the Sunday school and the maintenance of the church buildings. The young couple eagerly responded to the pastor's expression of trust in them and threw themselves into their ministries.

But as the extent of their responsibilities became apparent to them, they realized they had taken on too much. They were each spending more than twenty-five hours per week on church-related business. This was clearly more than the young couple and their now three children could afford.

Their ministries gave them status and made them feel like responsible adults, so giving up one or both of their positions was difficult to consider. Nevertheless, they made an appointment with their pastor to discuss their dilemma. After hearing their story, the pastor slumped disappointedly in his chair and said, "How could you let me down like this? I trusted you."

Stricken by these words—the same they had heard from their parents—Bev and Rob vowed to rededicate themselves to their ministries. They will most likely burn out in a few months and then have a second major failure to live down.

In many churches guilt manipulation is less obvious than this, but its purpose is the same—the control of vulnerable people. When believers accept performance-based standards preached by their leaders, they must keep the standards or suffer from guilt because they have failed. Either way, their behavior is manipulated and controlled. The genius of this system is that each religious group can custom-design its heavy loads to meet its own needs. In one place the standard is giving money; in another it is taking your turn at teaching Sunday school; in another it is serving on committees.

Even if a person has a powerful conversion experience with an afterglow of warm affection and devotion to God, he or she will wither spiritually under such loads. When the "first love" grows cold, guilt feelings intensify. It is not so much that love for the Lord has cooled, but that it has been weighed down and smothered by the joyless monotony of religious performance.

God's Load

Religious loads may be divided into three general categories. First there is "God's load"—that is, the law-keeping and the disciplines he supposedly demands of us in exchange for his approval and acceptance. Second is "our load." This is the idea that spiritual success is a do-it-yourself project: we must take care of our own sin and produce our own holiness. The third is "their load," the spiritual leaders' load.

This is when the burden of making our leaders look or feel good falls on our shoulders. Their load is the work we must do for their sake, to meet their needs.

Let's examine these more closely, beginning with God's load. The god of the Pharisees (then and now) is a cross between Santa Claus and a traffic cop. He's making a list, checking it twice (checking it *twice,* mind you), handing out fines to the naughty and rewards to the nice. This god supposedly requires each of us to take a standardized religious test. A passing grade earns his acceptance and favor; a failing grade results in his rejection or curse.

The fundamental theological problem with this system (for anyone who has read the Bible) is that the demands of God are not merely high—they are 100 percent perfection. A passing grade on his test is straight A's. The Bible also makes clear that none of us ever scores those A's: "For all have sinned and fall short of the glory of God" (Rom 3:23). So if God's acceptance of us is dependent on our keeping his laws, we are all equally lost—which is, of course, why we all equally need a Savior.

The law of God is invaluable to us not for divine acceptance, but to reveal divine judgment. "All who rely on observing the law are under a curse, for it is written: 'Cursed is everyone who does not continue to do everything written in the Book of the Law' " (Gal 3:10; see also Rom 12:12-13, 20; Gal 3:19). With God's law as our standard, we see the absolute futility of any and all self-effort justification.

But if law is held up to us as a hurdle to jump in order to get acceptance from God, it destroys us spiritually. Every Sunday at noon, thousands of well-exhorted saints march out of church with a renewed determination to die to self and live for God as they should. A week later they return, disappointed in themselves and ashamed. A few who are less honest or aware may feel pride in the previous week's spiritual accomplishments.

According to Larry Crabb, the problem of presenting Christian discipleship as discovering God's demands and working hard to fulfil them is that "our churches will eventually resemble first-century synagogues run by Pharisees ... filled with either weary folks who know that their best efforts fall short, but are willing to try harder next week, or proud people who, like their teachers, so badly miss the point of God's law that they think they are keeping it."[3]

One of the reasons that spiritual leaders tend to think they are keeping up with God's expectations is that they are the ones formulating those expectations. Over the years, pastors have taught the church to value the very things for which they are trained and have time, such as Bible study and prayer. Because their time is their own, they can go to any number of prayer meetings and spend hours in Scripture. A mother with young children or a business executive who commutes two hours each day cannot.

There is a kind of dehumanizing spiritual abuse that is actually worse than the misuse of God's law. It is expressed in the ill-defined calls to "enter into the deeper life," to "lay it all on the altar," to "surrender," to "yield" and so on. If these calls are not defined or explained, they can never be put to rest in our conscience. The question sensitive hearts perpetually ask is "Have I yielded or surrendered enough?" This establishes permanent guilt feelings and exchanges salvation by God's grace for salvation through my surrender, in which I can never rest.

The law is much less abusive, because at least it has definition. Reading the Ten Commandments, we can readily see which specific ones we have broken. But how do I know if I have ever surrendered all?

Archibald Hart tells a story that dramatically illustrates the cruel effects of these ill-defined exhortations to a higher spirituality. He once knew a young woman named Sonja, whom he describes as "extraordinarily talented," "self-confident," "considerate," "well-adjusted" and possessed of a "deep spiritual commitment and obvious love for her Savior."

Sonja fell under the spell of a Christian leader who adopted a very strict interpretation of Galatians 2:20 ("I am crucified with Christ"). He demanded that his followers "die" within themselves. Constantly hearing his exhortations to "die to self," Sonja tried. But she never felt as if she had totally succeeded. "Under this constant bombardment... Sonja plunged downhill fast." Unable to die to self spiritually, she finally walked to the railroad tracks, laid her head down on the steel rail and was killed as a train ran her over.

Hart concludes, "This true story illustrates how destructive faulty theology can be." True theology does not harm the self. If anything, it repairs it, upholds it and strengthens it.[4]

This is not to say that we should never exhort, never call people to deeper commitment. But when we do, we should take the advice of Bruce Narramore, who says, "We need to follow a motivational approach that communicates the fact that forgiveness and acceptance is the right of every person who trusts in Christ and that proper behavior flows from these rather than earns them."[5]

Religious manipulation that produces guilt starts out holding the carrot of approval in front of us but always ends up beating us with the rod of condemnation. If we continue to play the game of trying to carry God's load (100-percent perfect performance), we will finally collapse of exhaustion—or worse, as in Sonja's case.

God's Rest

Speaking to people like Sonja, Jesus says, "Come to me, all you who are weary and burdened, and I will give you rest. Take my yoke upon you and learn from me, for I am gentle and humble in heart, and you will find rest for your souls. For my yoke is easy and my burden is light" (Mt 11:28-30).

It is true that God demands much. In fact, his demands are more than we can deliver. The good news is that Jesus meets God's demands fully for us. Saints know that they have failed Christ. But they also know that he has never and will never fail them. As our Savior, he scores all A's on God's performance test, and as we believe in him, those scores are credited to us. We don't know how to worship perfectly, but he does. We don't know how to pray perfectly, but he does. We don't know how to trust and obey perfectly, but he does. We don't know how to love perfectly, but he *is* love.

If the sermons you listen to and the religious books you read burden and oppress you, chances are they do not reflect the ministry of Jesus Christ.

Jesus promises rest for all who are weary of trying to please religious leaders. He offers an easy yoke to all those laboring under a load of spiritual performance. If your religion is wearisome and burdensome, God's answer is not a longer quiet time, a firmer commitment, attendance at one more conference or one more trip to the altar. God's solution for spiritual tiredness is rest—rest in the loving acceptance of Jesus and his perfect load-carrying work for you.

The apostle Paul is adamant that our relationship to the law (all the tests and expectations of God) is radically and permanently altered by the work of Christ. He says, "God made you alive with Christ. He forgave us all our sins, having canceled the written code, with its regulations, that was against us and that stood opposed to us; he took it away, nailing it to the cross. And having disarmed the powers and authorities, he made a public spectacle of them, triumphing over them by the cross" (Col 2:13-15). Jesus disarmed the demonic powers by canceling "the written code ... that was against us." By enforcing that written code, then, abusive preachers actually rearm those demonic powers against us!

Jesus kept God's written code in his life and destroyed it in his death. Not only did Jesus live out perfect discipleship for us, but in Christ, God has forgiven us our sins and canceled the very regulations that defined our sins. Our wrongdoing and the standard that exposed it are both nailed to the cross. That is precisely why "there is now no condemnation for those who are in Christ Jesus" (Rom 8:1).

There is no doubt that God intends to be God to us and that we come to him by his standards and on his terms (or we come not at all). But his terms are consistent with his nature, which is free, sovereign mercy and grace. His way of accepting us is not through our shouldering his load but by our accepting his grace. The heart of the good news is that God declares us righteous the moment we give up our own claims of righteousness and accept Christ's righteousness as our own.

False shepherds will always give lip service to this mercy and grace, but will then undermine it in the body of their teaching and in their actions. I have before me a copy of *Handbook on Christian Discipleship,* which is presently making the rounds of American and Canadian evangelical and fundamentalist circles. In it I read,

> Eternal life is not given to us on the basis of God's mercy. It is given to us on the basis of doing God's will. We are judged according to our works, according to the deeds done in our body . . . An overemphasis on the finished work of Christ can destroy, indeed has destroyed, the very fiber of Christianity. Make no mistake, it is the conqueror who inherits eternal life. God takes no pleasure in fearful and undecided people.

Contrast this with Paul's statement that our salvation "does not depend on man's desire or effort, but on God's mercy" (Rom 9:16). And that "Christ is the end of the law so that there may be righteousness for everyone who believes" (Rom 10:4). Good shepherds will not only preach grace but will also practice it as they lift God's load from our shoulders in the strong name of Jesus Christ.

Our Own Load

The second type of load abusive shepherds lay on our shoulders is our own load of sin. John Bunyan's Pilgrim (in *The Pilgrim's Progress*) is the classic example of a man burdened down by his own sin; he carries it on his back like a great weight.

Pharisees then and now are able to load us down with our sins because of the way they define sins—or should we say the way they *list* sins. Spiritually abusive systems define sin as external behaviors. These behaviors are then written in lists. In some circles these lists might define proper versus improper dress and manners. In other circles the lists may focus on spiritual disciplines, attitudes and speech.

Defining sin strictly as external behavior is necessarily unfair and abusive. It creates a performance-based class structure in which the strong succeed and the weak fail. The "saints" carry their sin burdens gracefully while the "strugglers" carry theirs disgracefully, for the "saints" are able to deny and hide their sins while the "strugglers" (or the honest) cannot. Such a system gives the upper class an opportunity to boast and the lower class an occasion for shame.

Defining sin in terms of lists of behaviors was a point of conflict between Jesus and the Pharisees. Jesus repeatedly objected to the unfairness of such lists. More important, he objected to their shallow and dangerously misleading nature. Defining sin as external behavior trivializes sin and trivializes the person and work of the One who saves us from our sin. Michael Horton explains,

It is indeed a piece of irony that those who are constantly telling us what sins to avoid and how to avoid them actually have a low view of sin! But it's true. This was the case in Jesus' day. The Pharisees, you will recall, subscribed to a perfectionistic program. And to make their calls to perfection stick, they had to view sin as external—as actions rather than attitudes basic to fallen human nature.[6]

According to the Bible, however, the sin that separates us from God is first not in our actions but in our hearts. It is not first our behavior that needs correction, but our inner being that needs the cleansing of forgiveness and radical healing. Paul understood the unfairness of defining sin as lists of behavior. He also knew that the sin we need to be saved from goes much deeper than deportment. He also understood that to try to suppress sinful conduct with rules is utterly futile.

Since you died with Christ to the basic principles of this world, why, as though you still belonged to it, do you submit to its rules: "Do not handle! Do not taste! Do not touch!"? These are all destined to perish with use, because they are based on human commands and teachings. Such regulations indeed have an appearance of wisdom, with their self-imposed worship, their false humility and their harsh treatment of the body, *but they lack any value in restraining sensual indulgence.* (Col 2:20-23)

Note that Paul says not that rules and regulations are not enough to suppress sin but that they are utterly useless and "lack any value" in restraining sin.

Donald Sloat explains part of what is wrong with thinking of sin as external behaviors: "The trouble is that any list can be followed no matter how severe it is because it does have an end to it and can be mastered. A person who follows the list begins to believe it is possible to reduce the inner sinful state by reducing certain external behaviors. In other words, the focus is on the manifestation of sin (the list) and not on the inner state of being."[7]

For Jesus, sin was first of all an inner state of being with external behaviors as symptoms. Or as he explained to the Pharisees on one occasion, "Sin is not what goes into a man; sin is what is already in a man" (my paraphrase of Mt 15:11).

Sin defined as a list of dos and don'ts not only misses the essential point but also fatally misleads. First, there are always a few who think they have actually kept the rules. These see no need of a savior and so do not enter the door of the kingdom (Mt 23:13-14). Those who believe that salvation can be attained by the observance of rules and regulations but know that they fail to keep them also have the door of God's sovereign grace slammed in their faces.

In order to help the Pharisees (and us) understand the true nature of sin, Jesus explained that the adulterer is not just the one with the adulterous conduct but the one with the adulterous imagination (Mt 5:28). In Matthew 23:25 Jesus told the Pharisees that though they cleaned the outside of the cup (their external conduct), their inner beings were no less greedy and selfish. And though they looked white-washed on the outside, inside they were full of death and putrefaction (Mt 23:27).

The Pharisees thought "God helps those who help themselves." Jesus drove home the truth that God helps those who confess they cannot help themselves. "Blessed are the poor in spirit," he said, "for theirs is the kingdom of heaven" (Mt 5:3). Jesus constantly pressed for a radical definition of sin that denied any cure through self-effort. As long as we try to justify ourselves in terms of a list of dos and don'ts, we evade contact with the God who justifies the unrighteous.

Once the list of external behaviors is replaced by Jesus' definition of sin, we all fall to the same level of absolute poverty. Abusive class systems are dismantled, spiritual hierarchies are destroyed, and we all see our equal need of a savior. This is, of course, Jesus' point, and so, again, he says, "Come to me, all you who are weary and burdened, and I will give you rest. Take my yoke upon you and learn from me, for I am gentle and humble in heart, and you will find rest for your souls. For my yoke is easy and my burden is light" (Mt 11:28-30).

If you are worn out trying to keep your fears, compulsions and sins under control, Jesus' first answer to you is not more discipline or Scripture memorization, it is rest. Rest in his loving acceptance, and rest in his power.

There remains, then, a Sabbath-rest for the people of God; for anyone who enters God's rest also rests from his own work, just as God did from his. Let us, therefore, make every effort to enter that rest. (Heb 4:9-11)

For it is God who works in you to will and to act according to his good purpose. (Phil 2:13)

Our competence comes from God. He has made us competent as ministers of a new covenant—not of the letter but of the Spirit; for the letter kills, but the Spirit gives life. (2 Cor 3:6)

The Leader's Load

The third type of burden abusive leaders lay on people's shoulders is their own load. That is, they use us to meet their personal or professional needs. They manipulate by guilt, social pressure and "prophetic words" to ensure that people serve them. The classic example of this from Reformation history is the indulgences sold by the Roman pope to cover the cost overrun of building St. Peter's Cathedral. The pope offered pardons for sins in exchange for a contribution to his building fund. An agent from Rome named John Tetzel was reported to have played on the ignorance of the common people by chanting to them, "When the coin in the coffer rings, a soul from purgatory springs."

Closer to home, I know of a congregation that was tricked into building its pastor an expensive home in an exclusive neighborhood. The men in the congregation gave up weekends and holidays to finish the work. The pastor convinced the congregation that the Lord demanded this kind of service to their "delegated authority" (namely, himself).

A friend recently told me of a so-called healing service conducted in the church he attends. The visiting minister promised that on a particular night miracles would occur, and he specified the "healing of deaf ears." As a result of this promotion, many deaf people attended that evening. When the meeting had run its course and nothing much happened (and no deaf ears were healed), the visiting minister asked the congregation to join him in silent prayer. After a moment of quiet, he spoke solemnly to the congregation: "I just saw in a vision that God stood ready to heal every deaf person in this room, but you fell just short of the holiness he requires. So the Lord stayed his healing hand." The people had been cruelly manipulated to come to the meetings in the first place, and then they were shamelessly used to cover for the minister's failure.

A pastor I know helps to lead a Christian group that values corporate prayer meetings above any other church activity. In order to look good to his group, he believes he has to get his people out for the church's numerous intercessory prayer meetings. He gives status to those who regularly attend these meetings and denies status to those who do not. He also preaches that those who now pray sacrificially will soon be rewarded with high rank in God's end-times army. Again, people are being manipulated to meet the leader's needs.

I know another pastor whose church has not grown numerically in over twelve years. Frustrated by his manifest lack of success, he turned to the congregation to meet his need. He has laid on them a building program in hopes that a new, larger, more attractive facility will draw more people. The congregation has split over this issue. Many have left the church, and those who remain are now saddled with a crippling debt.

In each of these cases, the church leader looked at those he was responsible to protect and serve, and decided to make them serve him instead. Rather than meeting their needs, the pastor makes the parishioners meet his needs.

In Ezekiel 34, a passage I examined in chapter three, God judges the abusive shepherds in Israel because they took care of themselves rather than devoting themselves to the care of the flock (v. 3). Here and elsewhere in Scripture, God makes it clear that shepherds are supposed to be there for the sheep, not the sheep for the shepherd. Woe to the shepherd who abuses the sheep by acting to the contrary!

Abusive shepherds tie up various heavy loads and lay them on people's shoulders. Good shepherds take off those loads.

Tough Questions

After hearing me talk about these issues, a number of pastors have asked me how they could ever keep their people in line, keep them from sinning or keep them giving if all these loads were removed. They are asking, in effect, "If there isn't at least a little law to keep people in line, won't they run wild?"

My answer (from experience) is, "Yes, some may run wild. But at least then we know what we're dealing with—that is, unregenerate hearts."

There are many people in our churches who have never been renewed by the Holy Spirit, who have never in fact been born again. For one reason or another they simply took on the loads of Christendom and conformed their behavior to the expectations of Christian culture. It is important to find out who these people are so that they can be properly evangelized and birthed. Then and only then can they take on Jesus' easy yoke and light load and serve him in holiness out of love.

Other questions need to be asked. If we are leaders, we should determine our motives for seeking positions of authority. Do we assume leadership of others to fulfill God's call in our lives? To serve people? Or is pastoral office a means of achieving significance or gaining something else we lack?

Congregations, too, should ask their leaders questions that are designed to get straight answers. Every congregation has the right to ask their pastor and other officials just what their motives are for seeking church leadership. These congregations then should look hard at the evidence (the fruit) of the leader's life and ministry to see if it fits with his or her stated motives.

*It is not who you actually are but who people
think you are that matters.*
Joseph Kennedy

*Early in the 20th century, in fact in the onset of the Victo-
rian era, manners began to replace morals. . . .
This trend came in time to mean that corrupt manners
which repudiated Christian faith and morals
began to dominate popular culture.*
R. J. Rushdoony

*Everything [the Pharisees] do is done for men to see. . . .
Woe to you, teachers of the law and Pharisees,
you hypocrites! You clean the outside of the cup and dish,
but inside they are full of greed and self-indulgence.*
Jesus Christ

5
THEY DO IT
FOR SHOW

*I*t is human nature to want to look good for others. Some Christian leaders and organizations, however (like some politicians and political parties), seem absolutely preoccupied with their public image. When the church places manners before morals and appearances over reality, it becomes what Jesus spoke against in Matthew 23:5-7, 25-28. When leaders distort the truth and manipulate the weak for appearance's sake, they become abusive.

I recently received a letter from Romania which illustrates the abuse that is possible when Christian groups focus too much on their image. The letter was an invitation to come to Romania to conduct Christian conferences. Not knowing me (except through a book I had written), the Romanian pastor who wrote the letter felt it necessary to lay down some ground rules. He explained that since the revolution,

Romania had been inundated by representatives of Christian organizations wanting to hold large meetings there. Their main aim in doing so seemed to be public relations. They took pictures and produced video footage for their contributors back home. "But they did not seem to care for us at all—only their reputation as an international ministry."

Stretching the Truth

When I was young in Christian ministry, I founded an evangelistic street mission in the heart of a large West Coast city. I financed this work through the support of several local churches. The mission proved to be effective in reaching young people who were abusing drugs and alcohol. A number of these (some with dramatic testimonies) gave their lives to Christ. I featured the most impressive of these testimonies in my reports to our supporting churches. Churches were excited by our success, and I looked good in their eyes. This encouraged me to write even more striking reports of our successes, while downplaying (or omitting entirely) our failures. So while not technically lying about our work, I projected a distorted image of it.

My growing desire to look good for our supporters gradually affected my treatment of our volunteer staff. On the days we were visited by our supporters, I put our staff out on the streets, talking to people and looking busy. Even if they had other important activities planned, I made sure that they performed for the sake of appearances.

When I began to feel guilty about the way I was acting, I went to see the senior pastor of one of our supporting churches. I wanted to confess and get counsel. After telling my story, I waited for a rebuke or maybe a word of forgiveness. Instead he stared at me with a puzzled look and said, "So, Ken, what's your point? We expect optimistic reports. No one in ministry tells the unvarnished truth. We automatically take exaggeration into account."

If what he said is true, then the church regularly lies to itself and condones using people for its public relations needs. No wonder the world is leery of us.

I'm now actively involved in healing ministry, mostly in teaching people how to pray for the sick. I often hear how sick people are manipulated and used by a few so-called faith healers. It is common in some healing ministries to coerce people into claiming a healing that has not actually occurred. Others blame the lack of a healing on the sick person's defective faith. In these cases the victim of sickness is revictimized by a leader who is desperate to look good. For the sake of appearances, people get abused.

Making Denial an Art Form

A more common version of the same story is the pastor who berates the church, blaming them for low attendance at services or poor support for the church programs. Rather than look at the defects in his or her own leadership, the pastor focuses attention on the flaws of the congregation. Such a person is more interested in keeping up appearances than in discovering what is actually wrong.

There is one variety of abusive leader who is so preoccupied with keeping up appearances as to utterly deny human weakness and the depth of human fallenness. This is typically a very "positive" person— always smiles, always up. This pastor's sermons are full of easy answers and glib advice; his or her own dark temptations, marriage problems, failures as a parent are never disclosed. The only personal struggle that is confessed is expressed in the past tense, so that we see how victory has been gained. Often this pastor has gathered a leadership core of "yes men and women" who never confront problems. Since the pastor is allowed to live in denial, no one else is allowed human weakness either. Such denial suffocates honesty and fosters abuse.

The people in this pastor's congregation soon understand that in the life of the church there is no time for them to disclose their sin, no place to get ministry for their pain. There is no one to help shoulder their burdens. Thus the entire congregation is finally co-opted into the minister's denial of reality.

Living in denial is destructive and lays the groundwork for even greater problems. For instance, when the partners in a troubled marriage get the impression that it is more important to look good than to be honest, they hide their torment and struggle on in isolation. Cut off from the human comfort and spiritual resources of the church family, their marriage slides closer to the abyss.

When a dysfunctional family sees that there is no room in the church for their imperfections, they cover them. They put on smiles and act out the unspoken doctrine that it's better to *look like* a Christian family than to actually *be* one. The pain goes unnoticed and untreated, making a bad situation much worse.

There will, however, always be desperate souls in these churches who disclose their pain and ask for help anyway. A pastor friend told me how he and his staff used to handle such people. He said, "When people came to us with serious problems, we always tried to fix them up and get them looking good as soon as possible. We discouraged 'deep sharing' and tried to skirt the real problems. When people had problems because they had been hurt by the church, we got defensive and put a lot of pressure on them to keep quiet. It was the old 'don't talk rule' you see in dysfunctional families."

All churches do not have the human resources or the spiritual and psychological skills to meet every need. But providing a safe place to disclose needs and have them received is a central mandate of the church and the very least we can do. Paul clearly calls us to "carry each other's burdens"; in this way, he says, "you will fulfill the law of Christ" (Gal 6:2). If we deny our burdens for the sake of appearances, they can never be carried by others.

Denial modeled by leaders and transmitted by followers finally becomes a way of life for the church family itself. When the congregation conspires to deny its defects in order to look good to outsiders, it begins to act like any other dysfunctional family.

Don't Talk

One of the most troubling abusive traits in the dysfunctional church or denominational family is the unwritten "no talk" rule. This rule implies that certain problems in the group must not be exposed because then the group might look bad and things would have to change. The "no talk" rule itself is among those things never talked about.

Allowing such deception and suppression to exist within a fellowship not only fosters numerous abuses but is a flat denial of the meaning of Christian fellowship. If there are certain issues—such as leadership, decision-making or how money is spent—which you cannot discuss with members of your church, you do not participate in Christian fellowship with them. What you share instead is a commitment to what Schaef and Fasell call the "addictive organization": "Communication in the addictive organization is frequently indirect. ... People who feel they have conflict with one another refuse to state their conflicts openly to the person concerned. They are also unwilling to discuss these conflicts in public settings. Instead, they avoid the significant parties and carry tales to others."[1]

Gossip is one of the most destructive evils in the church today, and it is significantly encouraged by the "no talk" rule. If issues cannot be talked about in legitimate ways, they will be talked about in illegitimate ways. What actually happens is the inappropriate venting of frustration. Though gossip temporarily relieves tension and fosters the feeling of intimacy, ultimately it poisons.

For leaders, gossip can also function as a means of control. Because these people are in the know, because they have their thumb on the pulse of the church, they can act as the authoritative clearinghouse for information. Depending on exactly what they say to whom about the group or individuals in the group, they can keep people confused or intimidated and thus under control.

Suppose a woman in the church has a legitimate concern about the senior pastor's authoritarian style of leadership. She first speaks to the pastor about it, and he ignores her. She then talks to others about her concern, and at this point the pastor perceives her as a threat. He then counters her perceived attack by gossiping about her to the key leaders in the church. He confides to them that in a recent marriage counseling session with her and her husband, the woman confessed a deep rebellion against all authority, especially male authority. As their pastor, he is of course very concerned about her "hatred toward legitimate authority," but this does account (he observes) for her current attack on him. She and her concerns are thus discredited, discounted and dismissed. She is also personally hurt, because she is now labeled as rebellious.

Pastoral gossip is one means of controlling the flow of information and maintaining power. Another effective means of information control is what one group refers to as "uplining." Uplining means that members of the group must bring all questions and concerns to the leader directly over them. They are never to discuss any problem with anyone other than this person. This leader is then to keep this concern to himself or pass it up to the leader above him. Such a closed system enables the leaders to control the flow of information and to silence any person or issue they choose to.

Healthy groups thrive on the free flow of information. Members have ready access to each other's opinions and concerns. Sick groups generally suffer from confused, defective or controlled communication. Arterburn and Felton explain, "Communication in a toxic faith system isn't a two-way interaction. Information is valid only if it comes from the top of the organization and is passed down to the bottom. . . . Anything that doesn't fit into what they already believe to be true will probably go unheard."[2]

The inability to tolerate freedom of expression, honest questions and straight talk is a hallmark of an abusive system.

The Call to "Unity"

Another abusive result of the "don't talk" rule is that when people from inside the group finally break the silence and begin to talk about the group's problems, they are persecuted. They are told that everything was just fine until they started causing trouble. (Incestuous families react in exactly this way toward the first daughter to blow the whistle on her father and her family.)

If the whistle-blowers reveal the group's problems to the outside world, the group will mobilize to discredit them. Sometimes trumped-up countercharges are aired, but most often the troublemakers' mental and emotional state is brought into question. Almost never are the actual issues raised ever admitted, let alone dealt with. The real problems are not acknowledged; instead, the whistle-blowers themselves become the problem. Thus honest examination is averted and denial maintained.

This is what recently happened to a friend of mine. As he began to publicly question his denomination's doctrinal errors and ministry abuses, he was stonewalled by the leadership. Instead of responding to his very specific, unambiguous complaints, denominational leaders began to speculate publicly that he was acting aggressively because he felt hurt or neglected by them. Some said he had always had a problem with authority. Others who claimed to know him well wondered aloud if he was acting out of hurt from his childhood. Some of his fellow pastors went so far as to lobby a local newspaper to drop an article he had written. They felt that his critique (accurate and fair though it was) undermined "church unity."

A shallow appeal to unity is a common ploy of abusive groups. It often works, however, because no one wants to be accused of bringing disunity in the church. We all long for unity in the body of Christ. Even the angels long for it. But as Gene Edwards says, "Beware of the leader bearing an inordinate dose of unity."[3] Abusive leaders often appeal for unity in order to protect themselves from critical examination. A survivor of an abusive group put it this way: "I am tired. Tired of being bullied and seeing others bullied and persecuted all in the name of unity. I'm tired of representing an organization that has such frail faith in itself that it can tolerate no dissension in its ranks, not one bit of constructive criticism of the policies forced upon Christians by a dictatorial group of men."[4]

Any call to unity must be examined critically. Is it true Christian unity or unchristian uniformity that is being called for? Real unity is mutual submission which is freely and voluntarily given moment by moment. It is never coerced. If unity is defined as everyone agreeing with the leader on every issue, we have the uniformity of a dictatorship, not the unity of everyone submitting to one another out of reverence for Christ. If the unity called for includes keeping quiet about deep-felt concerns, it is not true Christian unity and we need not submit to it.

Phylacteries, Big Bibles and Unctuous Voices

The Pharisees of Jesus' day were preoccupied with a desire for uniformity among their followers. They attempted to impose a uniform orthodoxy in belief and practice through the law. Jesus blew the whistle on their abusive practices. This freedom that Jesus took for himself enabled him to prophesy the painful but necessary truth about them. Pointing out their neurotic need to look good to each other and the public, he referred to the show they made: "Everything they do is done for men to see: they make their phylacteries wide and their tassels long" (Mt 23:5).

The phylactery was a little black box containing a portion of Scripture. A Pharisee strapped one to his forehead to publicly demonstrate his devotion to the law of God. The idea behind the phylactery came from Deuteronomy 4:6-8, where Moses commanded Israel to impress the commands of God on their hearts, tell them to their children, tie them as symbols on their hands and bind them on their foreheads. These instructions to tie the laws of God to hands and forehead are, of course, beautiful Hebrew metaphor. In the case of tying God's law to our hands, we are to allow God's law to inform the work of our hands, to guide our actions. The meaning of tying God's law to our foreheads is obviously to let God's law educate our minds and guide our decision-making.

To reduce this beautiful metaphor to a black box strapped between one's eyes is to utterly miss the point. And the Pharisees missed it in a conspicuous and comical way. They not only strapped the box on their foreheads but enlarged it to demonstrate their superior piety. Symbols of devotion rather than devotion itself were (and are) important to Pharisees.

The modern equivalent of enlarged phylacteries depends on the fashion of a particular religious group. All such symbols and practices look silly, of course, to anyone outside the group. For some fundamentalists the widened phylacteries would be the big black Bible of the proper version, dog-eared and marked up. For another group it might be an affected manner of speech or lacing one's conversation with "Praise the Lord." For some it might be the wearing of a suit and tie; for others, jeans and a T-shirt. Examples are legion.

My favorite religious affectation that is employed to project piety is what I call "preacher's voice." Some preachers deliberately alter the timbre and tone of their voice when they ascend the pulpit (to sound more like the voice of God, I guess). It is as if they are playing the part of a servant of God rather than simply being one.

The widening of phylacteries is done for show, of course. Most such religious fads are merely comical or irritating and should be laughed at or simply ignored. But they are also danger signs. Making so much of external signs of devotion may indicate that authentic spiritual life on the inside has died or is dying. Widened phylacteries also demonstrate that the person wearing them is far too concerned with how he or she looks to others. When such people gain power, they become dangerous and are not to be trusted or followed. If ever they are forced to choose between their own image and the real needs of others, the latter will always lose.

In Matthew 23:25 Jesus discloses the danger of those who work hard to look good while neglecting spiritual integrity. "Woe to you, teachers of the law and Pharisees, you hypocrites! You clean the outside of the cup and dish, but inside they are full of greed and self-indulgence." These are leaders who shine themselves up for Sunday services; they set the standard in doing the forms of worship, but inside there is only death. Many of these pathetic souls are trapped in the abusive systems they created for others. There is now no place for them to talk about their spiritual dryness and death, and no one to help carry that burden.

Places and Titles of Honor

Jesus continues his exposé of the Pharisees by pointing out their need for "the place of honor at banquets and the most important seats in the synagogues; they love to be greeted in the marketplaces and to have men call them 'Rabbi' " (Mt 23:6-7). It would be fine if everyone had a seat of honor at a banquet at some time in his or her life. There is nothing inherently evil about our honoring one another, but the Pharisees *demanded* honor. They desperately needed to be recognized as honorable men—the very thing they were not.

Jesus' portrayal of their hypocritical desire to appear honorable reaches comic proportions in Matthew 6. Here Jesus pictures the Pharisees announcing their alms-giving with trumpets so that they can be "honored by men" (v. 2). They pray for show too: they stand in conspicuous spots in synagogues and draw attention to themselves on street corners "to be seen by men" (v. 5). Jesus warns against such shows, telling us "not to do . . . acts of righteousness before men, to be seen by them" (v. 1). And when we pray, we are to find a private place and "close the door" (v. 6).

In Matthew 23 Jesus rebukes the Pharisees' lust for honor, but he often scolded his disciples for the same sin (Mt 18:1-5; 19:27; 20:9-16; 20:28). "The desire to be number one, to be considered great is the most frequently combated desire in the gospels. . . . *Greatism* is exposed by Jesus in Matthew 23 as the principal source of false faith."[5]

The Pharisees' need for honor and their longing to be seen as great are demonstrated in their love for the greeting "My Great One," which is the literal meaning of *rabbi*. The modern equivalent of rabbi would depend on the specific religious group. In some groups, "My Great One" might be "Pastor" or, better yet, "Senior Pastor." For others, the title "Dr.," "Reverend," "Bishop" or "Elder" would show who is number one. Such titles set the titleholder apart from the common folk, which is of course the reason for them.

I know church leaders who train everyone (including their family members) to refer to them in public as Pastor Ted or Dr. John. This training, I suppose, is calculated to add reverence or honor to their position. It is my belief that a leader's need for a title in order to enhance his or her authority is in direct proportion to the lack of true authority. The demand for special status indicates a lack of real confidence. This may be why Jesus forbade such honorific titles and status labels.

> But you are not to be called 'Rabbi,' for you have only one Master and you are all brothers. And do not call anyone on earth 'father,' for you have one Father, and he is in heaven. Nor are you to be called 'teacher,' for you have one Teacher, the Christ. The greatest among you will be your servant. For whoever exalts himself will be humbled, and whoever humbles himself will be exalted. (Mt 23:8-12)

I cannot imagine language any more clear or forceful. If we take Jesus seriously here, we will all have to rethink how we address our leaders.

More literally and contemporaneously, verse 8 reads, "Don't you ever be called Doctor, Reverend or Master, for you have but one Master and you are all brothers and sisters." This is the clearest possible rebuke to all hierarchical religious structures. Jesus is radically committed to absolute parity within his church.

He continues, "And don't you ever call anyone on earth Father, for you have one Father in heaven." That is to say, even if someone demands to be called Father, Doctor, Pastor or Reverend, you refuse to do so. Such a radical social leveling of all God's people before the Father turns the church into a single household of God, which of course is its whole point (Eph 2:19; 1 Tim 3:15).

Along these lines, it is instructive to note how Paul uses the offices and titles of "bishop" and "deacon" in his letters. For instance, in Philippians 1:1 Paul omits the definite article when addressing bishops (or overseers) and deacons. This strategic omission means that the titles *overseer* and *deacon* describe their specific pastoral service or ministerial function, rather than their office. In other words, their titles indicate what they do for people rather than their position in the hierarchy. In his commentary on this verse, Ralph Martin states, "There seems to be general agreement that here the words [overseers, deacons] describe not the holders of ecclesiastical office but a responsibility which was assumed."[6]

Jesus clearly forbade the use of ecclesiastical office titles, but if Paul can be trusted, we may use them if and when they denote a function. We *should* use them when omitting them would be awkward or draw attention. For instance, when a woman in my church introduces me to her mother, she can hardly do so without referring to me as her pastor. When applying for credit or a course in graduate studies, it may serve a legitimate purpose for me to say that I have a doctoral degree.

Jesus is not saying that in his household there should be none who function as spiritual fathers, mothers, elders, theological doctors, teachers or leaders. Rather, he is saying that titles that describe our functions of service should never be used to elevate us above others or to oblige our brothers and sisters to regard us as "great ones."

Paul picks up this theme in Philippians 2: "Do nothing out of selfish ambition or vain conceit, but in humility consider others better than yourselves.... Your attitude should be the same as that of Christ Jesus: Who, being in very nature God, did not consider equality with God [or the title] something to be grasped, but made himself nothing, taking the very nature of a servant" (vv. 3, 5-7).

No matter how much we feel the need of offices or symbols of authority to improve our image and bolster our confidence, Jesus will not allow them. The only way to greatness in the kingdom of God is through humble service. And this seeking greatness through humble service alone has eternal consequences. "For whoever exalts himself will be humbled, and whoever humbles himself will be exalted" (Mt 23:12). According to Dale Brunner, "The two future passive verbs in this sentence—'will be humbled,' 'will be exalted'—refer to verdicts of the Last Judgment."[7] So even if humble service is not rewarded now, it will be then. And even if spiritual abuse is not judged now, it will be then. (See also Mt 16:27.)

Turns of Phrase

Abusive leaders parade their piety and lust after positions, titles and offices because they do everything "for men to see." Yet another tool insecure leaders use to enhance and defend their image is language. Abusive leaders often use words deceitfully and self-servingly. They do not speak to communicate but rather to confuse, manipulate and intimidate. "Woe to you, blind guides! You say, 'If anyone swears by the temple, it means nothing; but if anyone swears by the gold of the temple, he is bound by his oath.' You blind fools!" (Mt 23:16-17).

The false teachers of Jesus' day claimed to know the inner mind and workings of God above and beyond what is plainly revealed in

Scripture. In Matthew 23:16-22 Jesus violently denounces all religious language that is tricky, obscure, arcane, gnostic, esoteric or complex. Theological writers are sometimes guilty of posing as gurus who are uniquely capable of wielding such language. Today we also have "prophets" claiming divine revelations of heaven, principalities and powers, and the hidden purposes of God to which mere mortals do not have access. "Faith healers" tell us that they know the trick of finding which prayers God answers for particular illnesses. Men and women posing as Bible teachers claim to see much, much more in the text of Scripture than a plain, uncomplicated reading of it could ever yield. Whenever religious leaders claim special knowledge of God or the Bible which is hidden from the rest of us, we may be in the presence of false and abusive teaching, or something worse.

Abusive leaders also use language to confuse us and throw us off track when they feel themselves threatened. Sooner or later they will say something that is patently absurd and easily discredited. Rather than admit their error, they use words to slip and slide away from public accountability.

A minister recently claimed that his salary was $70,000 per year. It was later disclosed that remuneration for his ministry was close to $500,000 per year. When asked to explain the discrepancy, he said, "Oh, I was earlier referring to my actual salary. I was not including my housing, car, entertainment, medical and retirement benefits."

For years now we have heard predictions and prophecies of imminent worldwide revival. When the revival doesn't come as promised, the leaders who wrongly predicted it often devise creative ways of denying their error. Leaders from an internationally known ministry recently predicted that a big revival would start in a particular country during a specific month and that they would be instrumental in it. The month came and went, and nothing even vaguely resembling a revival broke out. Instead of admitting their error, the leaders spoke evasively. They said, "Even though it didn't look as if revival happened, it really did. The revival began internally in a few key people by spiritually renewing them. The full-blown revival will come later."

This amounts to redefining and distorting the church's accepted definition of revival; it was a cover-up to protect an image. It is very much like saying, "If anyone swears by the temple, it means nothing; but if anyone swears by the gold of the temple, he is bound by his oath." Such evasive doubletalk obscures truth to protect an image.

The truth of a matter is usually self-evident to sensible people. But if that truth conflicts with the personal or institutional agenda of abusive leaders, they often say what they need to in order to obscure it. Spiritual leaders possess the power to obscure truth not just because of their inherent authority, but also because most of them are skilled in communication. We want clergy to communicate skillfully, and we reward them for that skill. But that valued skill, when employed in one's own defense, may become a tool of abuse. A friend of mine rightly says, "The one with the microphone gets to tell the story." The combination of good communication skills and the authority of the platform is potent.

Grandma Sophie once told her precocious grandson Allen, "The smarter you are, the better your reasons for doing the wrong things."[8] The smarter we become as communicators, the easier it is to do wrong and make it sound right.

The Ambition of a Servant

It is my firm belief that those who flaunt their devotion, promote their position and posture their power do so out of basic insecurity. The man or woman who is confident needs nothing for show, needs no slippery or evasive speech to promote or defend self. Therefore, when Jesus says "The greatest among you will be your servant" (Mt 23:11), he is not calling us to paralyzing, humiliating self-negation or self-abasement. He is simply describing what secure, God-affirmed leaders look like and how they act.

A healthy leader may very well have high self-esteem and be very ambitious. Such a leader, however, will demonstrate that ambition in seeking greater and greater opportunities to serve. Even Jesus' ambition to serve all of us—to become the greatest Servant of all—was based on a quiet confidence in who he was.

Jesus *knew* that the Father had put all things under his power, and that he had come from God and was returning to God; *so* he got up from the meal, took off his outer clothing, and wrapped a towel around his waist. After that, he poured water into a basin and began to wash his disciples' feet, drying them with the towel that was wrapped around him. (Jn 13:3-5)

If we are going to be like Jesus, we may be ambitious—and we may be successful. But our success will be measured not by how many people we control but by how many we openly and honestly serve. We cannot wash feet while standing on a pedestal.

*The real test of religion is, does it make wings to lift a man
up or a dead weight to drag him down? Is a man
helped by his religion or is he haunted by it? Does it carry
him or does he carry it? ... The Pharisees believed
that to do God's will was to observe their thousands of petty
rules and regulations and nothing could be further from
the kingdom of God, his basic idea, his love.*
William Barclay

*Woe to you, teachers of the law and Pharisees, you
hypocrites! You shut the kingdom of heaven in men's faces.
You yourselves do not enter, nor will you let those
enter who are trying to.... Woe to you, teachers of the law
and Pharisees, you hypocrites! You give a tenth of your
spices—mint, dill and cummin. But you have
neglected the more important matters of the faith—justice,
mercy and faithfulness. You should have practiced
the latter, without neglecting the former. You blind guides!
You strain out a gnat but swallow a camel.*
Jesus Christ

6
MAJORING ON MINORS AND MISSING THE POINT

A *young minister had recently* come to serve a church I was attending. He was married with three small children. Not knowing how much it cost to live in the city where the church was located, he had accepted the church's financial offer without question. Once in the city with his wife and children, he realized that his agreed-upon salary was woefully inadequate. So at a church board meeting, he asked the chairman of the board to place his family's financial needs on the evening's agenda. Following an opening prayer, the chairman introduced the minister's concern as the first agenda item.

After the young pastor explained how his family could not survive on his current pay, the chairman quickly moved that this important matter be brought up at the budget meeting—to be held nine months later. The motion was carried without discussion, the issue was dropped, and the meeting moved on. The discussion of the young pastor's request for help had taken exactly six minutes.

The next item on the agenda took up the balance of the meeting (two and a half hours). That item was a new security system for the church buildings. The congregation owned several expensive office machines, and the board members felt the present security system was not adequate to protect these assets. So the chairman proposed that several thousand dollars be spent to upgrade the system. The money was allocated and the work scheduled immediately.

At this meeting, a young minister and his family were dishonored and trivialized. They finally had to leave the church. But the church's photocopier is secure.

This travesty of righteousness is a classic example of majoring on minors. According to Johnson and VanVonderen, "In a spiritually abusive system, the mundane becomes essential, the vital trivial and the real needs of people are neglected for the sake of agendas."[1]

This story also illustrates that spiritual abuse is not always perpetuated by the professional clergy, and that the victims of abuse are not always laypeople. It may work the other way around, depending on who has the power. In many churches, the so-called clergy have the power. But in some "congregational" or elder-led churches, the so-called laypeople have the power. In the latter case, they have the potential to abuse the hired minister.

Neglecting Weighty Matters

In Jesus' day, the spiritual power class was the Pharisees. A hallmark of this group was their preoccupation with trivialities and their blindness to major issues of righteousness. When Jesus confronted these ecclesiastical point-missers, he said they were scrupulous in tithing even the herbs they grew—mint, dill and cummin—yet they neglected justice, mercy and faithfulness (Mt 23:23).

Tithing, or giving a tenth, was (and I believe still is) the proper thing to do. Jesus himself tells the Pharisees that they should continue it. The tithe was, in fact, commanded by God (Lev 27:30-33) and blessed by God (Mal 3:6-12). Nevertheless, tithing is a relatively minor issue in the Bible, while justice and compassion are stressed on almost every page.

Ancient and modern Pharisees, while emphasizing minor religious matters, may cheat in business, brutalize wives and children, and be indifferent to the poor and impatient with the socially backward. They can adhere to minor points of the law while they take oaths and break them. In the modern spirit of ancient Pharisaism, men can wear the right clothes to church, give money, pray faithfully, become skilled in Scripture and yet neglect the truly important matters of the kingdom of God.

There are many women who do not miss a single meeting of the church; they are perpetually available to teach Sunday school and serve on committees. The husbands of these "dedicated" women often feel rejected by them, and their children are lonely for them at night.

Majoring on minors and missing the point.

Straining Out the Gnats
Spiritually abusive leaders and systems characteristically invert spiritual values. Uncompromising stands may be taken on matters of no spiritual significance, while issues of greatest importance are minimized. Or as Jesus so graphically put it, "You strain out a gnat but swallow a camel" (Mt 23:24).

To the conscientious Jew, both gnats and camels were unclean and must not be ingested (Lev 11:4, 42). To avoid swallowing a gnat when they drank wine, the Pharisees strained their drink through muslin gauze. If no gauze was at hand, they strained their wine through their teeth, picking the gnats out of their teeth with their fingers. But, says Jesus, while the Pharisee is careful to protect himself against a microscopic speck of impurity, he gulps down a ton of defilement (humps and all) and never even notices. This is Jesus' vivid portrayal of a leader who has lost all sense of proportion, whose spiritual values have become completely inverted.

Not long ago I took a group of pastors from my city to a conference I was conducting in a nearby town. Following the conference, we all went out to dinner with the pastor whose church had hosted us. When he ordered wine with the meal, I cheerfully drank two glasses. One of the pastors who had come with me returned to our city and began warning others that I had a drinking problem. A few months later it was disclosed that he had been cheating on his wife for the previous three years.

Straining out gnats and swallowing camels.

Another pastor of my acquaintance had a reputation for enforcing a meticulous dress code in his church services. The choir robes had to be pressed each week, the men serving Communion had to dress in dark suits and black ties, and any visiting preacher had to wear a white shirt and black tie under a black robe. This same pastor contracted AIDS through homosexual practice.

Another pastor I knew made much of the fact that he never used the church's envelopes or stamps to mail his personal letters. He stated this to me on at least three occasions. This same man was later fired for stealing cash from the offering plates, which were stored in his office between services.

More gnats and camels.

The conflicts that the Pharisees initiated with Jesus were usually over minor issues. They disputed with him about fasting (Mk 2:18), sabbath-keeping (Mk 2:24), eating with unclean hands (Mk 7:1-5), eating with unclean people (Mt 9:11), attitudes toward taxes (Mk 12:13-15) and so on.

They majored on minors in disputes with Jesus because, as we have seen, religious minutiae were their passion. By contrast, Jesus had a passion for God's in-breaking kingdom and how this kingdom benefited real flesh-and-blood people.

The Pharisees were upset that Jesus repeatedly healed sick people on the sabbath. A conservative reading of the Old Testament sabbath laws supported their concern. Jesus, however, treated sabbath observance as a minor issue compared with someone's immediate need. Without specific Scriptures to support his actions, Jesus healed sick and demonized people on the holy day.

When the focus of a ministry moves away from pastoral needs toward religious protocol, programs or budget, it is entering a potentially abusive mode. Real people and their real needs are always the major concern for Jesus. Religious correctness is always a minor issue to him.

Pharisees fret over spiritual trivia. They lay picayune religious burdens on themselves and others. Jesus' "religious instruction," on the other hand, is given in only the most general terms. Jesus gives us no systematic code of religious behavior like those left by Moses, Buddha and Muhammad.

Moreover, Jesus comments little on social morality. He says virtually nothing at all about politics, relations between the sexes and relations between nations. His silence on these issues allows us freedom and scope. Unlike the Pharisees, Jesus has no interest in setting up rigid religious and social guidelines for his followers. He chooses instead to major on the significant agendas of the kingdom of God.

The Door of the Kingdom

When Jesus initiated conflict with the Pharisees, he focused on the most major issue imaginable. In Matthew 23:13 he accuses them of nothing less than keeping people from God: "You shut the kingdom of heaven in men's faces. You yourselves do not enter, nor will you let those enter who are trying to." Jesus majored on majors and drove straight to the point.

This accusation against the Pharisees is crucial because it, more than any of the others, demonstrates how completely they missed God's purposes in their religious fervor. It is a crucial accusation also because, if it can be brought against any modern church leader, it means that leader has also tragically missed God and denied him to others. I cannot imagine a more serious charge.

How exactly did the Pharisees slam the door of the kingdom in people's faces? First of all, while Jesus calls these "door closers" hypocrites, we should not think of them as knowingly hypocritical. There may have been some charlatans and con artists among them, since these are usually present within every religious group. But on the whole, the Pharisees were like the religious elitists of every age. They sincerely thought that they were serving God and doing it better than anyone else. Yet Jesus accused them of actually working for the enemy.

The most obvious way that these leaders kept their followers from the kingdom of God was by turning them against the King. "It was the Pharisaic leadership that diverted Israel from Jesus and so kept Israel from the kingdom of heaven that was breaking in through Jesus."[2] This is the sin against the Holy Spirit which will not be forgiven (Mt 12:22-32).

The Pharisees did not want to be identified with Jesus and his new community, and they worked hard to hinder others who were attracted to him. Wanting to keep their position as the gatekeepers (ruling on who was in and who was out of God's community), the Pharisees naturally rejected Jesus, who proclaimed himself the new gatekeeper: "I tell you the truth, I am the gate for the sheep" (Jn 10:7). Jesus made clear that he would not only replace the Pharisees as the gatekeeper but also completely do away with their traditional understanding of the gate. Anyone who wanted to come in was welcome, sinners especially (Mk 2:17).

In Luke 17:20-21, the Pharisees ask Jesus when the kingdom of

God would come. Jesus answers, "The kingdom of God is among you" (NRSV). The kingdom of God which all pious Jews anticipated was already breaking in upon them, all around them, and they were missing it by rejecting the King. Majoring on minors, they had missed the point.

To compound this tragedy, they were working hard to see that others missed it too. Matthew 23:13's parallel verse, Luke 11:52, makes this even clearer. "Woe to you experts in the law, because you have taken away the key of knowledge. You yourselves have not entered, and you have hindered those who were entering." But by God's grace they were not altogether successful. On another occasion Jesus tells the Pharisees, "The tax collectors and the prostitutes are entering the kingdom of God ahead of you" (Mt 21:31).

According to George Eldon Ladd, "The kingdom of God stands as the comprehensive term for all that the messianic salvation included."[3] This "messianic salvation" included (and includes) forgiveness for sin, right standing with God, healing, deliverance, social justice and more. To deny any of Christ's messianic salvation is to close the door of the kingdom to some degree.[4]

A second obvious way the Pharisees slammed the door to the kingdom on themselves and others was by misunderstanding and misrepresenting the law of God. Instead of teaching the law as God's liberating gift to a fallen people in a fallen universe (which was the proper Old Testament perspective), they burdened people with the law. They interpreted and taught it as legalistic minutiae, thus obscuring the true kingdom of God.

The third way they shut the kingdom of God in people's faces (and this has the widest modern application) is by making it cost something. To put it bluntly, the kingdom of God that breaks into our lives through the Lord Jesus Christ is offered to us free. Regarding salvation, God deals with us strictly on the basis of his mercy and his grace. He refuses to sell us anything. Jesus, through his life of perfect obedience and sacrificial death on the cross, secured our entrance into the kingdom and our continuing good standing in it. We may receive all of God's blessing in Christ freely, or not at all.

Since Pharisees (then and now) are committed to working for standing before God, they do not receive it. And if they convince others to work for it, they deny it to others. "You travel over land and sea to win a single convert, and when he becomes one, you make him twice as much a son of hell as you are" (Mt 23:15). Such abusive pastors are "blind and foolish guides" and are not to be trusted or followed. Majoring on minors and missing the point can be deadly for followers as well as leaders.

Responding to Abuse

This brings us finally to the most troublesome and controversial problem of all. When we think that we may be under the "care" of blind and foolish guides, what should we do? The answer is not always simple. Some whose judgment is limited by immaturity or skewed by past wounds will jump ship too soon. Others, out of a false sense of loyalty or fear of missing God's blessing, will stay in an abusive situation when they ought to depart. Between these two wrong extremes there is a way of discernment and good judgment.

In the first place, if a member of a congregation believes the pastor is acting abusively, Matthew 18 says that member must go and confront the pastor. Then the process of church discipline should be allowed to run its course, if possible. We will study this in some detail in chapter ten, "Healthy Church Discipline."

One legitimate response to spiritual abuse may be to remain in the situation for a time. Some independent and mature saints may be called to stay and pray, awaiting the pastor's repentance or departure. Some people will feel that they have invested far too much in a church to allow a blind guide to destroy it.

A friend recently told me of a congregation that dwindled to eight persons under an abusive priest. Two who stayed were a husband and wife who continued to pray for the renewal of the priest and the church. As the denomination finally began proceedings to close down the church, the pastor had an "experience in the Holy Spirit," as they said. This experience radically changed his ways—which, of course, affected the church. The congregation soon began to grow in size and influence, and today it stands as a leading light in its denomination. The couple who stayed had a true spiritual call, and such calls are valid.

We must also consider all abuse, spiritual and otherwise, on a continuum. I suspect that all churches (and for that matter, all people) are abusive to some degree. All of our institutions are made up of fallen and sinful people. Abuse may come by passive neglect or by active manipulation, but we all treat each other with less than perfect love. In assessing abuse and deciding what to do about it, we need to discern it in terms of degrees. Some minor abuses we ought to overlook entirely; some we need to confront and forgive; others we must flee from.

If a friend embarrasses me with a cutting remark, I should probably shrug it off, especially if it is uncharacteristic of him. I should not major on that minor issue. Moving up the continuum of abuse, I may yell at my kids or neglect my wife. In such cases, they should call me on it and I must repent. Moving close to the top of the spectrum, a man may systematically beat his wife and rape his teenage daughter. In this case, both wife and daughter must get out and report these crimes to the police.

Some neglect and rudeness should not be called abuse at all; the term is too loaded. That would be majoring on a minor. If someone says, "My father was abusive because he once gave me a spanking I didn't deserve," the term loses all meaning.

In discerning and assessing abuse in church, we must not think in perfectionist terms. Once a year the pastor may put a little pressure on the congregation to meet the budget. This might indicate insecurity or lack of faith on his part, but to call it spiritual abuse debases the real thing. If every sin prompted by insecurity is abuse, then nothing is. So at the low end of the continuum, some minor manipulation and rudeness ought to be offered up in prayer and forgotten.

Moving up the scale, we all ought to step in and confront one another on significant hypocrisy. All of us, either in home or church, do not always "walk our talk." Since we each have an incredible ability to rationalize our own inconsistencies, we need them pointed out to us. As a pastor I may say, "God has no favorites and neither does this church. We are all equally accepted in Christ." Yet I may prefer those who are effective in serving the church or making me feel good. In this event, someone needs to call me on it and I should repent.

Farther up the scale, we find churches which have become "significantly aberrant Christian organizations" (SACOs, for short). These are groups, churches and parachurch organizations that adhere to mainstream Christian doctrine but practice almost total control over the decisions and actions of their members. Ron Enroth offers case studies of such groups in his book *Churches That Abuse.* Those who find themselves caught in a SACO should probably make a run for it. Such groups are usually so well defended against criticism, so completely in denial, that to attempt to confront them would only cause more harm to the confronter.

To sum up, I would say that if abuse is minor and rare, we should probably shrug it off. If it is significant, we should confront the perpetrator. If it is systematic, ongoing, unrelenting and well defended, we probably need to leave.

Spiritual abuse does not often present itself in black and white. It usually shows up on the gray (middle) part of the continuum, and assessing it is not always easy. If we become too idealistic in our search for a perfectly nonabusive pastor or church, we will wander from place to place, never finding a home. Majoring on minors is dangerous not only for leaders but for followers too.

Sometimes an abusive person seizes a position of power in an otherwise nonabusive church. If we are hurt by someone like that, we need not indict the entire group because of it. On the other hand, good leaders may have inherited a basically abusive church system which they have not yet had time to change. Such leaders should be able to count on our support. If we do not allow for such situational considerations, we will lock ourselves into a kind of perfectionism that places intolerable demands on leaders. Depriving them of mercy and grace then becomes *our* contribution to the church's load of spiritual abuse.

Why It's Hard to Get Out

Over two decades of leadership in the church and on the mission field have shown me, however, that the mistake most people make regarding ecclesiastical abuse is not leaving prematurely but staying too long. We will go into this in the chapter entitled "Who Gets Hooked and Why." For now, let me simply explain something of the subtle and paradoxical nature of abuse which often makes it so difficult to criticize and escape from.

First of all, abusive spiritual leaders gain followers because they are, in one way or another, attractive. Their attractiveness may very well be their genuine commitment to the work of God and their sincere desire to train mature disciples. The intention to maim people may not be present in them at all. I know several pastors whom I consider to be significantly abusive. I know them well enough to say that they are not deliberately abusive. Members of their congregations recognize their sincerity regarding the things of the Lord and so continue to support them, and thus continue to absorb their abuse.

We must be clear, however, that leaders' good motives should not permit them to continue hurting people. After all, the Pharisees whom Jesus opposed were also intensely sincere toward God. They loved God and his Word. They worshiped him. They thought they were pleasing God by teaching others what they sincerely believed. But a person may be as devastated by a well-meaning father as by a sadistic criminal.

There is a street ministry on the West Coast of the United States which targets urban drug addicts, alcohol abusers and prostitutes (both male and female). The gospel its staff members preach is mainstream evangelical. Their converts receive ongoing spiritual counsel and practical help such as temporary housing and job placement. This all sounds good, but there is a significant price paid by anyone accepting help from this ministry. In order to receive resources from this group, a person must give up freedom of conscience and personal decision-making. The leaders of the ministry control the lives of their followers almost totally. They dictate to them what they are to think and say, what they may wear, whom they will marry and where they can live.

When the leaders are questioned about their "oppressive authoritarianism," they explain that they are only doing what love requires. "Street people," they say, "have no self-discipline, so discipline must be imposed on them." They may appear benevolent because of their work among the most troubled people in our society. But it can also be said of them that they victimize those people by making them permanent dependents.

Such well-meaning abusers must be confronted, and if possible, stopped. We should expect, however, that they will probably not see or admit to the harm they are doing. There is a curious innocence in these leaders. They act with cruelty without having any conscious aim of doing so. They usually don't want to hurt people. Ironically, what they do want is, on the surface, good—evangelism, commitment to the mission of the church, respect for authority, church growth, mature discipleship, a balanced church checkbook. They can't see that they become abusers in the pursuit of these good aims. If they give any acknowledgment at all of the abuse, it's often minimized. "After all," they say, "I am seeking first the kingdom of God." They fail to realize that they are actually closing the door to it.

This paradox of ecclesiastical abuse shows up often at the institutional level. A Christian organization may profess biblical aims while spiritually ruining its members. An institutional commitment to "community outreach" or "support for foreign missions" may impoverish and dehumanize people, depending on how those commitments are kept. Like a well-oiled machine, such an institution grinds on year after year. Because its goals are right, most people (especially its victims) find it awkward to criticize. Thus it continues to secure the consent of its members, even those it hurts most.

Yet another paradox is the dual nature of abusive people. A parent can be cruel and abusive one moment and full of good humor and kindness the next. Wives who are beaten by their husbands often tell me how repentant and attentive the husband is afterward. Episodes of kindness give false hope and so keep the victim frozen in place.

As it is in families and marriages, so it is in churches. Moments of genuine caring and concern from the pastor keep church abuse victims hanging on. Even the most hardened abusers somehow sense that people will not put up with them forever, so (out of guilt or guile) they learn the art of episodic kindness, or what psychologists refer to as intermittent reinforcement.

So when we assess the integrity of a Christian leader or group, we do not look first at its motives, its aims or its moments of kindness. We look first and last at its fruit. If leaders constantly root their authority in an office rather than in servanthood, if they do everything for show, if they demand special privilege or titles, if they use words deceitfully, if they major on minors to the neglect of real pastoral needs, and if this behavior tears people down rather than builds them up, then such leaders must be confronted and changed—or abandoned.

Regardless of what we decide to do in response to real and actual spiritual abuse, there is one essential thing we must do: we must forgive the abuser. In this, too, we follow Jesus' example. For in spite of Jesus' harsh words to the spiritual abusers of his day, he stood ready to forgive them: "O Jerusalem, Jerusalem, you who kill the prophets and stone those sent to you, how often I have longed to gather your children together, as a hen gathers her chicks under her wings, but you were not willing" (Mt 23:37). He forgave everyone, especially those who abused him. In several places in the New Testament Jesus insists that we follow him in forgiving those who do evil against us. "For if you forgive men when they sin against you, your heavenly Father will also forgive you. But if you do not forgive men their sins, your Father will not forgive your sins" (Mt 6:14-15).

The significant abuse we suffer in the family or the church may be extremely difficult to forgive because the perpetrator is someone in authority, someone who should have protected us. Betrayal augments abuse when a person in high position violates our trust. The deep pain and damage suffered are unlike any other. When the beloved becomes the beloved enemy, we are stretched to the end of ourselves and beyond by Christ's command to forgive (Mt 5:43-47). At such times we must go to God, asking him for the power of the Holy Spirit to do what he commands. "You will receive power when the Holy Spirit comes on you; and you will be my witnesses" (Acts 1:8). Should we fail to forgive, the hell we plunge into is even more painful than the abuse we suffered (Mt 18:32-35).

If we decide initially to stay in an abusive relationship, we must do everything we can to secure repentance from the abuser as we fully offer forgiveness. We have to be clear that if we are to have anything like Christian fellowship with those who have hurt us, they must at some point acknowledge their sin and repent of it. No true relationship between Christians can exist without this cleansing. We can forgive without their repenting, and this will free us from the bondage of ongoing bitterness, but we will not have a reconciled rela-

tionship with them until they repent.

At a Bible school where I once taught, the wife of one of my colleagues asked me for help with her husband. She said that he occasionally physically and sexually violated her, and she asked if she should leave him. I said that we must first make every attempt to get him to change. "If he refuses," I said, "you have my support in leaving him."

She explained that she had done what she could to get him to change by repeatedly confronting him with his sin and expressing as graphically as she could how it wounded her. I asked, "How does he respond to that?"

She answered, "He shrugs and says, 'If you were a real Christian, you would just forgive me.' "

I asked, "What do you say?"

She answered, "I say, 'Yes, of course, I want to forgive you and I will forgive you, but we first have to talk about it. You must see what you are doing to me, and you must stop it.' "

If we stay in a situation where we have been abused, we have to talk about it with the perpetrator. Sooner or later, we must come to some agreement on it. If change results, then repentance has occurred. Only then is true Christian fellowship possible. If not, we may have grounds to leave.

We now turn to examining more carefully who gets hooked by abuse and why; what causes leaders to fall into patterns of abusive behavior; and what makes their followers put up with it.

*When a person's sense of self-worth is blunted, he
will deflect towards power to find fulfillment. . . .
That person will look to power over people
to lift his own self-worth.*
Viktor Frankl

*Toxic faith is a destructive and dangerous relationship
with a religion that allows the religion, not
the relationship with God, to control a person's life.*
Stephen Arterburn & Jack Felton

*You know that the rulers of the Gentiles lord it over
them, and their high officials exercise authority
over them. Not so with you.*
Jesus Christ

7

WHO GETS
HOOKED
AND WHY

*I*n modern Western society, where no one is legally or socially compelled to attend church, spiritual abusers need the voluntary "cooperation" of their victims in order to function. In this chapter we will consider why some people voluntarily submit to spiritual abuse. At the same time, we will gain insight into why others become their abusers.

This is, of course, a huge subject. An entire volume is needed to treat it comprehensively. In an attempt to set boundaries around the topic, I have chosen to draw mostly upon my own experiences and observations. This helps me limit the discussion, but it poses other problems. Some readers with their own experiences and deep convictions will wonder why I gave attention to one issue while ignoring another. Others will think that I missed the most important point altogether. Some will think that I dealt poorly with subjects that I didn't intend to deal with at all. So let me reiterate: what follows is not intended to be a comprehensive treatment of the subject. The convictions I express are based on personal pastoral experience and observation.

What type of person is attracted to the abusive leader? In my experience, the victims have often been unwittingly groomed for such a relationship. That is to say, something in the backgrounds of these people predisposes them to submit to a manipulative, controlling style of leadership.

Karen's Story

The story of a young single mother who attended our church for a short while is a striking illustration of how some people are groomed and prepared to submit to authoritarians. Karen came to us with a host of emotional and financial needs. We responded by placing her in a supportive home group, paying off most of her pressing debts and fixing her car. While she expressed gratitude, it was clear that kindness was foreign to her; our love and acceptance made her uncomfortable.

My preaching, which generally emphasizes God's gracious acceptance of us in Christ, was also a problem for Karen. She told her home-group leader that my sermons were "unbalanced" and did not represent "the full counsel of God." The following Sunday after the service, she stopped me at the door and, trembling with rage, demanded to know why I was so "soft on sin." She wanted to know when I was finally going to preach on "holiness, commitment and dying to self."

I feebly responded with something like "Well, I guess I can't say everything in one sermon." At that she spun around and marched out, and has not returned.

As it happened, she was seeing a counselor who is a friend of mine. He asked her permission to fill me in on her background. She gave it and he did.

Karen grew up in what we would call a dysfunctional and abusive home. Her father was a drunk, her mother a tyrannical perfectionist. Karen's mother made unrealistic demands on her and then punished her for failing to meet them. Her mother wanted Karen to have "religious values," so she sent her to a local church noted for its moralistic teaching. At this church, Karen learned something that predisposed her to spiritual abuse in the future. Her pastor and Sunday-school teachers convinced her that if she worked hard enough at "Christian" virtues, God would bless her. Karen, desperate for God's acceptance and her church's approval, did work hard. She performed especially well in Sunday school and earned many stars after her name on the class roll.

Despite her earnest, conscientious efforts, Karen's life did not improve but got worse. Her father's drinking became even more intolerable; her mother's harshness deteriorated into sadistic cruelty. Karen's religious performance had obviously not produced the promised blessing. Instead of concluding that there was something wrong with the works/blessing formula or that her religious leaders were in error, Karen concluded that the fault was hers—she had not yet done enough. Instead of giving up, she vowed to do even more and try even harder. Somehow she clung to the erroneous hope that if she was good enough, God would one day smile on her.

If she had learned the gospel of God's free grace and that she is accepted by God simply because Jesus makes her acceptable, she might have been spared a great deal of grief. She might also have been able to escape the clutches of spiritual abuse later. As it was, her self-doubt combined with her concept of God as an angry perfectionist led her from one authoritarian church to another, searching for a way to do enough to gain God's approval.

Karen's fundamentalist religious education gave her a moral conscience. This internal conviction of right and wrong conflicted sharply with the sin she fell into in her early teens. Karen's need for affection and acceptance, which her home and church failed to fulfill, was partially met in sexual relationships. In the struggle between human need and religious conscience, human need won out (it usually does).

Each time her emotional void was temporarily filled through sexual encounter, she felt even more lonely, ashamed and defective because she had sinned. She believed God had good reason not to bless her. Instead of giving up, she was spurred by her guilty conscience to attempt even greater religious performance. Karen became a living contradiction—as my counselor friend said, "a walking civil war." She was habituated to religious activity and sexual sin at the same time. The emptiness in religion drove her to the affirmation in sex, which in turn drove her back to religion to atone for her sin. Over the years I have spoken to dozens of Christians (mostly clergy) who are caught in this same addictive cycle.

Karen got pregnant at the age of sixteen and married the father, who was eighteen. In time he became the same sort of abusive alcoholic her father had been. When his drinking became dangerous, Karen took her two children and moved from the Midwest to southern California. That is when she got involved with our church.

After her brief stay with us, Karen began attending a church in our area noted for legalism and an authoritarian leadership style. Karen felt strong enough at this point to try once again to live the holy life that she thought would eventually make her OK with God. The church's list of dos and don'ts and its drive to control her life gave her a track to run on.

The Shame Motivation

There are many like Karen who have become convinced early in life that God is a despotic perfectionist. A lack of acceptance at home and in the church often drives them to religious performance, the very thing that abusive leaders and churches always demand. If they are never touched by the gospel of radical grace in Christ, they remain susceptible to religious manipulation all their lives.

Sometimes shame-based motivation to religious performance is intensified by a particular sin, real or imagined. As one man of my acquaintance grew up, his parents and his church told him often that he was destined for the public ministry or the mission field. When he graduated from college, he went into business instead. Although he became quite successful, he remained haunted by the fear that he had missed "God's will" for his life. The resulting guilt and shame drove him to overcompensate by giving the church all the money it asked for and by serving on every committee it told him to. His compulsive religious performance transcended any realistic notion of Christian service. His need to atone for an imagined sin matched perfectly his church's authoritarian demands. This was how he was hooked by spiritual abuse.

I know a high-profile Christian minister who masturbates compulsively. No one in his church or denomination knows about it. All they see is a man who can not say no to anyone. Driven by shame, he vainly strives to get even with his conscience by making himself available day and night to the demands of his church and denominational leaders.

Those who were brought up to believe that God is a perfectionist tyrant will be vulnerable to leaders who call for religious performance as the way to please him. Others who suffer chronic guilt and seek to assuage that guilt through religious works are potential victims of leaders who will manipulate and control them.

The Insecure Abuser

I have observed two classic types of spiritual abusers. The more common type is the leader who feels insignificant and seeks significance by gaining dominion over others. He or she is plagued by inner doubts and fears. This person may have been personally wounded by spiritual abuse in the past and may grab power as a form of self-defense. There may be no conscious desire to hurt; the injuries to others are byproducts of this person's quest to "become somebody" while protecting him- or herself.

Power-seeking ministers attempting to compensate for a sense of inner weakness will often put their heel on the necks of those under their authority. Leaders who secretly think themselves unqualified often wield a heavier hand than those who are secure. Some lack a healthy sense of independence; their abusive tactics may stem from the prodding of a spouse, friends or denominational leaders.

Church leadership is attractive to these needy people because of the authority uncritically afforded them. The office of Christian leader carries with it the authority of "the man or woman of God." The prestige of Christian ministers has declined drastically in Western culture, but it is still significant in many circles. In no other occupation (except the military) can a person move into town and immediately gain significant influence over a large number of people. The pulpit allows preachers to enjoy undivided attention week after week without interruption or challenge. Beyond the derived authority of the pulpit, pastors hold power over others through their roles as spiritual adviser, counselor, administrator and CEO. They may also control significant sums of money. No wonder some develop into ecclesiastical autocrats.

When this powerful person is also very insecure, with a fear of failure and poor impulse control, he or she may prove dangerous. It is ironic but nevertheless widely acknowledged among counselors that abusers often share the same troubled histories as those they hurt. Someone like Karen may respond to her debilitating childhood experiences by gravitating toward people who perpetuate their own experience of abuse. Others with backgrounds similar to hers may respond by protecting themselves against future abuse and seizing the role of the controller. Since abusive relationships are all they know, they continue in that type of relationship but in a different role.

A friend of mine is the director of a large Christian counseling group. His staff of over thirty counselors sees hundreds of clients from dozens of churches each year. He tells me that it is easy for his group of counselors to track the churches in the area that are spiritually manipulating people. Once a week all the staff gather to report on the sessions with their clients during the previous week. Often several of them report meeting with different clients from the same churches and with the same problems. They have seen over the years that most legalistic, authoritarian and controlling churches produce the bulk of their caseloads. They have determined that troubled people often gravitate to the churches that exacerbate their emotional problems.

My friend also told me that the pastors of these abusive churches often come to him for help. He is impressed by the fact that the perpetrators of abuse usually struggle with the very same inner conflicts as those they hurt. As the cliché goes, "Hurt people hurt people." Hurt people in positions of power often misuse that power to control and manipulate those they feel threatened by. They do so to create a sense of order and personal safety.

I recall several years ago that I was tempted to fall into this very pattern. I'd been serving a large church as pastor. The congregation was well established and had traditionally been controlled by a board of elders. The elders and I differed on many issues, matters of ministry and policy which were important to me. I felt that they were thwarting my attempts to lead the church. (Again, it's clear that spiritual abuse does not always come from the pastor. It may come from anyone in any group that has power.) I would not classify the elders' handling of me or their rule over the church as extremely abusive, but it certainly was oppressive.

Following a particularly contentious elders' meeting, I vowed never again to put myself under the control of such men. Had I been more wounded or lacking in personal resources, I might have left that position and found a group where I could have functioned more as a

dictator. Fortunately, my next assignment offered much more freedom and a group of elders with whom I shared the same philosophy
of ministry. That inner vow was never acted on.

Healing for the Abuser

A friend who is a repented spiritual abuser told me how he became
one. He described his childhood as "religious but void of acceptance
or approval." When he left home, he searched for a place where he
could feel significant. He also wanted a job where people needed him.
He gravitated to the professional Christian ministry (an all too common story). He explained how in his first church he quickly gathered
about him those parishioners who met his needs, those who supported
him uncritically. "In time," he said, "I established a class system, with
my supporters at the top and those who posed a threat to my leadership at the bottom. This system aided me in the delusion that I was
doing the right things."

My friend then told me the pain and destruction he inflicted on
those at the bottom and how he trained those at the top to follow his
abusive style. He was finally delivered from his compulsion to control
others by a deeper understanding of God's mercy and grace. He has
now publicly repented and is seeking to undo the damage.

The gospel in all its truth and power is the only cure for the abuser
as well as for the Karens of this world. Until they encounter the real
gospel, they will seek and find each other. The person habituated to
receiving abuse needs the abuser as much as the abuser needs his or
her victims. The abuser needs someone to master; the victim needs
someone to master him or her. Victims think of themselves as deserv-
ing abusive treatment. Abusers see themselves as entitled to deliver
the mistreatment that the victims feel is due. When the abuser and
the victim find each other, they create a sick symbiosis currently
called *codependence.*

The abuser finds comfort in being God to someone. The victim finds security in being swallowed up by someone else's need. Neither may consciously want the pain that results. Pain is simply the price that must be paid. The payment, however, puts each participant more and more in debt. Only by declaring total and permanent bankruptcy and depending wholly on God's mercy and grace can either find life and dignity and a way out. Only by dying to the counterfeit comfort and security found in abusive, codependent relationships can each of them find true freedom and the right kind of independence. More about this in the next chapter.

The Narcissistic Abuser

The second classic type of spiritual abuser is the heroic, grandiose or messianic narcissist who is obsessed by a desire to be someone great or to do something unprecedented for God. Carrying out this fantasy requires the cooperation of others and access to their money. Like the first type, this leader may not consciously wish to hurt anyone; but others *are* hurt as they are used for the leader's and God's "higher purposes."

Sometimes the first and second category of leader combine in one person. The most obvious examples are the major cult leaders. In the political realm, a defective ego combined with a messianic complex and access to great power produces a Hitler, a Mussolini or a Stalin.

Like the first type of abusive leader, narcissistic abusers are very complicated. In some ways they are even more dangerous than the insecure abusers, because they appear so virtuous, so committed, so gifted and sold out to God. They are also more dangerous because they are determined not just to protect themselves but to have themselves worshiped. They want more than just a safe place for themselves: they want themselves glorified.

The potential for adult narcissism has roots in our childhoods. Most little boys (and I am told, some little girls) go through a narcissistic stage where they imagine themselves performing heroic feats for those they look up to. I know I did. I can vividly remember rehearsing in my six-year-old mind a dramatic rescue of my family and my first-grade teacher, Miss Trimble, from a burning building. Superman and Tarzan were my models. This is a stage that time and reality temper in most people.

But heroic leaders have never outgrown their childhood fantasies. The soul of the true narcissist has managed to withstand the process of maturation. Adult narcissists cling to the dream of one day doing something truly exceptional and unprecedented for adoring fans and for God. They fantasize about writing a bestseller that will change the course of church history, or evangelizing the nation, or establishing the one true church, or alleviating world hunger, or becoming a commander in God's end-times army. They have a grandiose sense of self-importance. They feel entitled to unlimited success. They believe that they deserve human adulation as well as divine favor.

Narcissistic leaders tend to devalue others in order to maintain their exaggerated sense of self-importance. They may become frustrated or annoyed at others' pain if it gets in the way of their own wants. Narcissistic leaders are not just cunning con artists. They really believe they are entitled to public greatness and that the needs of others around them are of no importance.

They are potentially dangerous because they need followers to applaud their vision and virtues and to justify their actions. Their greatest fear in life is being unimportant, nameless and faceless.

The most accessible platform for such a leader, sadly, is the pulpit. His initial session behind the pulpit may be the first time he ever experiences the attention and power he craves. If he is truly gifted and is willing to work hard, he sees the possibility of realizing his dream. When a measure of that dream is realized and the messianic leader finally tastes the power he craves, he wants more of it. It becomes a kind of addiction.

In order to achieve the public support he needs, these leaders often make extraordinary claims for themselves or have others make them in their behalf. Such claims may include a special anointing, unusual personal sacrifice, unprecedented encounters with God, unique training, a singular teaching or leadership gift, a revelation of truth that is not available to others, or secret knowledge of God's end-times purposes. These and other claims imply that God has a special calling on this leader, and so it is the "unspecial" people's duty to admire and follow him, which they often do in droves.

Messianic claims to greatness are often crude and straightforward, but sometimes they are more subtle. I recently overheard a messianic-type leader preaching to his congregation from Hebrews 13:17: "Obey your leaders and submit to their authority. They keep watch over you as men who must give an account." The essence of his message was that the church had to obey him and submit to him; otherwise he would have to give an account. If they did not obey and submit, he explained, God would judge him and send him to hell. I was not only amazed at his terrible exegesis and exaggerated sense of self-importance, but stunned that his congregation bought it! They left muttering to one another that now they really must try to become more obedient and submissive.

Once the leader's claims to specialness and importance are established, it becomes very difficult for mere followers to challenge him. In time this leader breaks free of all accountability. This enables him to act as he pleases while exercising control over followers.

But it's not always easy to keep control. People have needs of their own, and sooner or later they feel them and want them met. The messianic leader tries to keep them from acknowledging or expressing their needs by promising them something better in the future. In order to subvert them from living honestly today, he promises them, "Revival is just around the corner," or "The great move of God is just ahead." Keeping his followers out of touch with today enables him to continue operating in his own interest.

Another tactic of keeping people out of touch with the present is to foment confusion, punctuated by crisis. Policies may be handed down and programs launched which seem to fit no coherent pattern. Prophecies are given that conflict with the ones uttered last week, but no explanation is offered. The resulting turmoil keeps people from finding out what is really going on. This serves to cover up the fact that almost no productive activity may be occurring and that the little that does happen requires an inordinate amount of effort. Because no one (except those at the top) knows what is happening, gossip is rampant.

Crisis is sometimes needed to further muddy the waters. Enemies—demonic, political or ecclesiastical—are invented to promote an "us-versus-them" siege mentality. The leader often sounds as if his group is at war with the world. This keeps followers looking outward so that they will have no energy or will to examine their own painful emotions and broken relationships.

A most effective means of control for a messianic leader is to convince his followers that they are on an extraordinary mission with him. If a leader successfully convinces his followers that he is the unique instrument of God, that makes *them* unique by virtue of their support of him. This group may say or imply such things as "We are a special move of God," "We are the only group proclaiming truth," "We are the faithful remnant," "We are God's cutting edge for this generation," or "We are in training for God's end-times army."

Once this attitude is rooted in a group, the combination of pride and fear keeps followers in formation. Everyone wants to feel special, and some get hooked on the exhilaration of being part of an elite. Others fear leaving lest they miss God's will and be accused of deserting his special calling. This leads us to the question of who gets hooked by messianic leaders and who volunteers for the abuse they inflict.

The Narcissist's Followers

Most of us want heroes. We want someone who understands and is able to cope with a world that is so obviously out of control. We want a father or a big brother to lean on—someone to cosign for our lives. If we think we have found him, we will give him incredible power and latitude. We are likely to overlook his mistakes, rationalize his inconsistencies and excuse his sins against us. We may act as if it is a privilege to be used and misused for his noble cause. We would rather be compliant victims than be on our own and part of nothing important. The sacrifice of our individuality is a small price to pay for being part of his special group.

The young and idealistic are especially vulnerable to messiahs. They have lived long enough to know that the world, including their own lives, is a mess, but they have not lived long enough to realize that any solution is complex. The self-designated messiahs give easy, black-and-white answers to problems.

Youth who are conscious of their weakness gravitate to leaders who seem to possess wisdom and strength. They may feel powerless against temptation and sin and want someone to make decisions and prescribe boundaries for them. They want the true New Testament church, where things are done right. The immature want someone to be mature and certain for them.

Young people are also drawn to a cause. It may seem noble to them to submit to extreme religious demands in order to "make a difference." The idea of being one of God's chosen is intoxicating. But escape may be part of the attraction. Submitting to a cause, just like taking drugs or alcohol, is an escape from growing up and establishing a personal identity.

Lack of sophistication is also a hazard for the young and inexperienced. They have not had enough experience with people in general, and leaders in particular, to make good judgments about them. If a leader claims to know the answers and acts sure of himself, young people may believe him. If a messianic leader takes for himself the "seat of Moses," they may let him have it.

As previously noted, the messianic leader promises something in the future to subvert honest living today. Yet some of his followers' needs finally become so acute that they are forced to make a change. If they conquer their pride in being part of a spiritual elite and rise above the fear of missing God's will, they may still be kept in line by another force. They may reason, "I have already invested so much in this leader and group—I can't abandon my investment. Maybe in time it really will pay off, and it will all be worth it."

Continuing to invest in a loser is a common phenomenon. An investor who gets emotionally hooked by a stock may continue buying it even though it is doomed. Someone who has sunk a lot of money into a used car may continue to pay for repairs that cost much more than the car is worth. A wife or a child may cling to a relationship with an alcoholic or a drug addict in hope that one day he will snap out of it. In the same way, some followers continue to support a leader who hurts them; they hope against hope that he will finally deliver.

Unless there is conversion and repentance, such leaders never do make good on their promises. The only messiah who ever delivered is Jesus Christ. All the others disappoint.

Many Christian workers appear to equate guilt feelings with divine conviction. If we can be made to feel guilty, or badly enough about ourselves, they reason, the Holy Spirit has done (or is doing) his work.
Bruce Narramore

The Reformation was a time when men went blind, staggering drunk because they had discovered, in the dusty basement of late medievalism, a whole cellar of 1500-year-old, 200-proof grace—a bottle after bottle of pure distillate of Scripture, one sip of which would convince anyone that God saves us single-handedly. The word of the gospel—after all these centuries of trying to lift yourself into heaven by worrying about the perfection of your own bootstraps—suddenly turned out to be a flat announcement that the saved were home-free before they started. Grace was to be drunk neat: no water, no ice, and certainly no ginger ale.
Robert Farrar Capon

If the Son sets you free, you will be free indeed.
Jesus Christ

Therefore, there is now no condemnation for those who are in Christ Jesus.
The apostle Paul

8
HEALED BY GRACE

I *recently spent three hours* on a radio call-in show discussing spiritual abuse. During the session I outlined the material you have read in the first seven chapters of this book. The on-air calls I received dramatically confirmed the need of this study. All of the calls were from "survivors" of ecclesiastical abuse. Most wanted to know how to get over the guilt and shame that had set them up for abuse and how to be healed of the additional guilt and shame the abuse inflicted.

I responded by trying to apply some aspect of God's grace to each caller's specific need. To each one I affirmed, "The only cure for the abuser, as well as the abused, is a sufficient dose of God's mercy and grace."

Needing to sum up the interview after two hours and fifty-five minutes, the host of the program said, "So, Ken, what you are saying in a nutshell is that if we know for sure that we are really OK with God and other people because Jesus makes us OK, then no one can manipulate and control us ever again. And if the abuser realizes that he too is fully loved and accepted by God, he will never need to lord it over anyone ever again." He said it very well.

Driven by Shame

As we have seen, abusers and their victims are often driven to their roles by self-doubt and related pain. They describe this inner pain in various ways. Some feel indicted by a sense of personal defectiveness; others report a pervasive fear of punishment for not measuring up somehow. The term that probably best describes these internal states is *shame.*

There is an important distinction between *guilt* and *shame,* though some use the words interchangeably. Guilt is emotional punishment for bad behavior. It corresponds to something wrong that we did. Shame, on the other hand, indicts us for *who we are.* It is attached to our being. A severe sense of guilt prompts us to hate what we have done. This pain may drive us to repent and make restitution. A severe sense of shame, on the other hand, prompts us to hate who we are.

People respond to self-doubt, self-hate and shame in various ways. Karen, whom I described in the previous chapter, submitted to abuse from people and institutions because shameful feelings made her feel that she deserved abuse. Shame calls for punishment, which is exactly what abusive leaders offer.

Abusive leaders may feel deeply shamed themselves, but instead of looking for a punishing person to submit to, they look for people to lord it over. I have often seen leaders who feel personally defective and inadequate elevate themselves above others in order to get relief from their ill feelings about themselves. Gaining a position of superiority over others temporarily calms their self-doubt. Soon, however, they need another fix, so they continue seeking ways to exercise power over others. The illegitimate use of power is like drinking salt water. The more you drink, the more thirsty you become.[1]

In many abusive relationships, therefore, the common denominator between victim and abuser is shame. Shame invites abusive treatment by one and prompts abusive behavior by the other. If a solution for self-hatred and shame could be found, it would go a long way toward healing the abused as well as the abuser.

Shame and the Law

What is it that causes this deep, pervasive shame in so many of us? What creates the sense within us that we do not measure up, that we are not OK?

Counselors, theologians and sociologists give various answers to these questions. The answer I offer here is the one I believe the apostle Paul gives. Paul understood that the guilt we own and the shame we feel are related essentially to our sense of the law. Paul's use of the word for "law" *(nomos)* is complicated and much debated. For our limited purposes here, I follow the conviction of most New Testament scholars that Paul sees the law in at least two distinct and opposing senses—one positive, the other negative. C. F. D. Moule says, "It is clear that 'law' is used by Paul in the two quite distinct connections which may be called respectively 'revelatory' and 'legalistic.' "[2]

Paul sometimes presents the law as something good and helpful that reveals God's will for our lives. God's holy law, summarized and symbolized by the Ten Commandments, shows us how we are to relate to God and to others. In this sense, God's law is his gracious gift to us as we try to live in a fallen world. Thus Paul tells Timothy that "the law is good if one uses it properly" (1 Tim 1:8). The law may have a remedial function in that it prepares us for faith in Christ (Gal 3:19-25). Paul also believed that the law was needed to control the larger society (1 Tim 1:9). In this positive sense, "the law is holy, and the commandment is holy, righteous and good"; so "we know that the law is spiritual" (Rom 7:12, 14).

Yet Paul most often speaks of law in negative terms. This is true especially when he describes how we gain right standing with God and find freedom from guilt and shame. Before his conversion to Christ, Paul thought he had gained righteousness and deliverance from guilt and shame through his own keeping of the law. His encounter with the resurrected Christ included the blinding insight that his right standing before God had nothing whatever to do with his own efforts. His real righteousness and freedom from guilt and shame came as gifts of God's grace. He came to see all his own lawkeeping as rubbish so that he might gain Christ, "not having a righteousness of my own that comes from the law" (Phil 3:9).

The coming of Christ ended everything Paul had been taught about the law's role in making him right with God. Instead of finding righteousness through the law, he realized that living under it meant living cursed. "All who rely on observing the law are under a curse" (Gal 3:10). Paul saw that no one could ever really fulfill 613 commands and prohibitions completely. Thus the law made sinners of everyone.

Paul and those like him, who discount the law as a way of acceptance with God, are sooner or later accused of "antinomianism"—that is, being "soft on sin." The truth is exactly the opposite. Paul took sin too seriously to ever think it could be dealt with through human effort, no matter how heroic the effort. In Romans 5:6-10 we are described as "powerless," "ungodly," "sinners" and "enemies." Sin renders us totally incapable of pleasing God through our own efforts. The law by itself can never save; it can only condemn.

"While we were still sinners, Christ died for us. Since we have now been justified by his blood, how much more shall we be saved from God's wrath through him!" (Rom 5:8-9). And as we shall soon see, how much more shall we be saved from the wrath of a guilty conscience and deep-seated shame through him.

No matter how hard and how long we try to do right and be right, it never works. Shame is always at hand, and self-hatred is just around the corner. There simply is no way to earn acceptance and forgiveness. If these are to come at all, they come as free, unmerited gifts at someone else's expense.

As we have seen, Christ may put the law to profitable use. But Paul insists that it can never be used in a legalistic way to gain God's (or anyone else's) acceptance, approval or favor (Rom 10; Gal 2:16, 21; 3:13; Phil 3:9).

The Greek language in which Paul wrote had no words for *legalistic, legalist* or *legalism.* But when Paul speaks disparagingly of the law, he has in mind what we call legalism. Whenever the law (the written code, as in Rom 7:6 or Col 2:14) is used by leaders to manipulate their followers, it becomes the primary tool of spiritual abuse. Authoritarian leaders not only misuse the law but add to it their own "oughts and shoulds" to strengthen their control over people. To a shame-based follower, these laws become the internal principle of self-accusation.

Any voice (external or internal) which demands that we do more and try harder to merit divine or human approval is what Paul refers to as "the curse." Ron Enroth's study of abusive churches shows how effective legalism is for the purpose of cursing and controlling people through guilt and shame manipulation. He says, "Preoccupation with keeping Christian rules enhances guilt feelings in members and it acts as an effective control mechanism for power abusers."[3]

Freed from the Law

The gospel of Jesus Christ, properly preached and understood, is the only cure for the misuse of the law. The Good News is the only means of neutralizing legalism, the primary tool of spiritual abuse. When we see that we are completely accepted by God solely through the life, death and resurrection of Jesus, all religious law loses its manipulative power over us.

When Paul announces our deliverance from self-accusation and declares our freedom from the oppression of legalism, he often speaks of our death to the law. One of the most interesting and helpful instances of this is Romans 7:1-4. Here Paul says, in effect, that we were once married to the law and under the control of the law. Now, in Christ, we have died to that abusive spouse and married Christ, whose fruit we now bear.

In the motion picture *Sleeping with the Enemy,* Julia Roberts's character is married to a controlling, tyrannical, high-powered business executive. Like all conscientious Pharisees, he is obsessed with detailed performance. He demands that his wife hang the bathroom towels straight and that she perform perfectly in public. When she accidentally trespasses one of his rules (read "laws"), he verbally, emotionally and physically punishes her. His abusive power over her is virtually total and makes her life unbearable.

She must break free of him. Divorcing him is out of the question; he is too possessive and powerful to allow that. One of them must die if her freedom is to be secured, so she fakes her own death. Successfully accomplishing this, she flees to another city hundreds of miles away and assumes a new identity. By her "death" she apparently delivers herself from a life of torment.

If we stop the story there, we have an illustration of Paul's understanding of our death to the law.

Do you not know, brothers—for I am speaking to men who know the law—that the law has authority over a man only as long as he lives? For example, by law a married woman is bound to her husband as long as he is alive, but if her husband dies, she is released from the law of marriage. So then, if she marries another man while her husband is still alive, she is called an adulteress. But if her husband dies, she is released from that law and is not an adulteress, even though she marries another man. (Rom 7:1-4)

The background to this illustration of how the death of either husband or wife dissolves all legal obligation is found in Romans 6:14: "For sin shall not be your master, because you are not under law, but under grace." The law defines sin and indicts us of sinning. The law confirms our guilt and so seals our bondage to sin. As long as law is our master, we are subject to the constant accusation of being sinners. The only way to escape this oppression and the self-accusation that goes with it is to make a radical break from the law.

Paul explains that this happens through death. Possibly the most wonderful mystery of the gospel is that we are actually "in Christ" in his life, death and resurrection. We really do participate in his experience, even his experience of death.

We were therefore buried with him through baptism into death in order that, just as Christ was raised from the dead through the glory of the Father, we too may live a new life.

If we have been united with him like this in his death, we will certainly also be united with him in his resurrection. For we know that our old self was crucified with him so that the body of sin might be done away with, that we should no longer be slaves to sin—because anyone who has died has been freed from sin. (Rom 6:4-7)

"All the virtue of Christ's death in meeting the claims of the law becomes ours, and we are free from the bondservice and power of sin to which the law has consigned us."[4]

Paul's point is that law binds the living, not the dead, and we are dead. We are radically liberated from the tyranny of our first spouse, the law. We are now free to marry a new spouse and become subject to him. The fruit of our first marriage was sin and shame (Rom 6:14). The fruit of our second marriage is the character and works of God (Rom 7:4).[5]

The Nature of the Law

Let us now look more closely at the character of our old spouse, the law, to see why we so desperately need to break free of it. In the first place, the law speaks to us only when it is offended. It can relate to us only as an accuser. "Through the law we become conscious of sin" (Rom 3:20), "because law brings wrath" (Rom 4:15). The accusatory character of the law is consistent wherever it is found. When a traffic officer pulls us over, we know that we are about to be accused of a crime. The police never stop us to compliment our driving. When we receive notice of an IRS audit, it is not to find out what we have done right but what we have done wrong. Officers of the law contact us only to accuse, indict and punish. Properly handled, the law has a place in the Christian life and in society, but it makes an abusive spouse.

Another characteristic of this abusive spouse is that it never takes into consideration extenuating circumstances. There are times, due to weakness or ignorance, that we offend the law. That doesn't matter to this spouse. If we are wrong, for whatever reason, we must be punished. To make things worse, this cold, impersonal spouse is always right and we are always wrong. This spouse cannot be appealed to or negotiated with.

The worst aspect of being married to the law is that it never dies. We are never freed from it by its death, so if death is our only hope, *we* must die. The good news is that this is precisely what has happened in Christ. "Don't you know that all of us who were baptized into Jesus Christ were baptized into his death?" (Rom 6:3). "You also died to the law through the body of Christ" (Rom 7:4).

If a marriage is nullified by the death of one of the parties, then our first marriage to the law is void. Once we fully understand this truth in the literal sense, law as a tool of abuse is neutralized and the heavy loads drop off. When we deny leaders the manipulative use of law, we are on our way to recovery. That is not to say that recovery is always instantaneous. Some habits, including shame and vulnerability to manipulation, die hard.

The legalistic use of the law and the additional oughts and shoulds that stem from it are the bastard children of God's holy law and actually lead us away from God. "Legalism pulls us away from following Christ towards another gospel, another gospel that says the cross is not enough."[6] Legalism is the first of the loads Jesus seeks to lift off our burdened shoulders.

Dealing with Conscience

In 1967 I was drafted into the United States Army. As an army private, I was subject for two years to the authority of all who were higher on the military hierarchy. In the spring of 1969 I was honorably discharged, but I remained on base two days while I waited for transportation home. For those two days I was a civilian, free of military authority. But the previous two years had habituated me to subservience. Even as a free man I continued to defer to the authority to which I was no longer subject.

Many Christians say they have heard, understood and believed the gospel. But when they continue to subject themselves to the legalistic manipulation of spiritual abusers, we must assume that the Good News has not yet sunk in fully. For some this takes time. So we must continually reinforce the truth that we have in fact died to the law and are no longer obligated to it. Meditating on biblical passages which assure us of the radical nature of our acceptance by God through Jesus can be helpful.

Much of the law's abusive power is due to the nature of our conscience. Conscience is the internal voice that pronounces judgment on our motives and actions. It commends us for doing what we think is right and condemns us for doing what we think is wrong. Notice my wording: "what *we think* is right" and "what *we think* is wrong." The conscience functions much like a computer programmed by cultural values. If we program our conscience with the truth, it will judge us according to that truth. In this case, our conscience is of immense value to us. It is a kind of moral homing device. If, on the other hand, we program it with a lie, it will judge us according to that lie. As computer experts say, "Garbage in, garbage out." This is why we cannot always let conscience be our guide.

For the person who is fundamentally shame-based, the conscience is an open wound that does not heal. People who believe they are essentially defective find their conscience punishing them for almost everything they think, say and do. A skilled spiritual abuser armed with a code of religious oughts and shoulds can exercise great power over such a person. One who is already vulnerable to manipulation through shame is made more so as heavy religious burdens pile up.

The religious abuser, knowing how to exploit this vulnerability, will erroneously say or imply that it is the conviction of the Spirit. Such conviction can be relieved only by doing more and trying harder. If the leader says our problem is lack of submission, we submit even more. If the leader perceives our problem as a lack of prayer, we will pray harder. If the leader says we haven't given enough, we will dig deeper. The purpose of this manipulation of our guilt and shame is to get us to perform the way the leader wants us to. The big lie here is that relief from guilt and shame will come through our own self-effort. The carrot held out to us is the promise of peace. The stick held over us is the threat of a tormented conscience.

There are people who are immune to such spiritually abusive manipulation. One category is those who are impervious to pangs of guilt because their "consciences have been seared as with a hot iron" (1 Tim 4:2). With time, the hot iron of habitual hypocrisy will numb the sting of conscience.

Another category of persons who will not be affected by the condemnation of the written code is those like Job. Job was blameless, upright and perfect in all his ways (Job 1:1). Therefore, he could stand up to the torment of his accusing "friends," insisting,

    I will never admit you are in the right;

        till I die, I will not deny my integrity.

    I will maintain my righteousness and never let go of it;

        my conscience will not reproach me as long as I live.

    (Job 27:5-6)

Those of us who cannot assert our personal righteousness with the certainty and vigor of Job must find another way to defend ourselves from an accusing conscience and the authorities who seek to manipulate it. That other way is by understanding and acting out of our union with Christ. We who have believed in Christ share not only his death (as we have seen) but also his life. We participate in his resurrection life, which awaits us beyond the grave. We also participate in the merits of his earthly life (Rom 5:17).

Our earthly progenitor, the first Adam, sinned, and guilt, shame and death were the results. All of us born of Adam share in his sin and guilt and the judgment that follows. "In Adam all die" (1 Cor 15:22). But the last Adam, Jesus Christ, was born of a virgin and not Adam's lineage. He lived a perfectly obedient life before God and did not partake of Adam's sin. In fact, his life has radically reversed the first Adam's disobedience and its effects. As the rest of 1 Corinthians 15:22 tells us, "in Christ all will be made alive."

Again, the gift of God is not like the result of the one man's sin: The judgment followed one sin and brought condemnation, but the gift followed many trespasses and brought justification. For if, by the trespass of the one man, death reigned through that one man, how much more will those who receive God's abundant provision of grace and of the gift of righteousness reign in life through the one man, Jesus Christ. (Rom 5:16-17)

Adam's sin indicted all of us. To reverse this, the obedience of the last Adam, Christ Jesus, brought "justification." Therefore, when we intelligently receive "God's abundant provision of grace and the gift of righteousness," we may then "reign in life through the one man, Christ Jesus."

"Righteousness" (right standing before a holy God) is a gift of God's abundant grace to us. This gift has absolutely nothing to do with our performance, good or bad. Instead, it has everything to do with Jesus' performance. God's gift of righteousness to us means that the merits of Christ's perfectly obedient life are now credited to us. As we participated in the first Adam's earthly experience, we now share in the last Adam's earthly experience.

Among other things, this means that while we do not obey God perfectly, Jesus did, and in God's eyes, his success is exchanged for our failure. We do not pray, love, worship, forgive or suffer perfectly— but Jesus did, and his performance is credited to us. It is as if the straight A's on his report card were transferred to our report cards.

"Christ is the end of the law so that there may be righteousness for everyone who believes" (Rom 10:4). No longer can any law be held over us as a tool of shame. There really is absolutely no condemnation for those who are in Christ Jesus (Rom 8:1).

If we assure ourselves of this, the shame that makes us vulnerable to guilt manipulation is neutralized. Yes, we sin, and yes, we must live in daily repentance. But we repent not only for our sin and failure but also for our righteousness and success. It is not just our vices that need forgiveness but also our virtues, because all we do falls short of perfection. Our performance, good or bad, has nothing to do with God's acceptance of us. We are either equally saved in Christ or equally lost outside of Christ. Grasping this good news frees us from debilitating shame.

Paul says that we must "keep hold of the deep truths of the faith with a clear conscience" (1 Tim 3:9). And keeping hold of these deep truths of faith actually clears our conscience. A clear conscience is God's gift to followers of Jesus and a sign of their mature understanding of their organic unity with Christ. These are people who, according to David Seamands, are "by faith receiving the perfections of Jesus Christ, so that perfection is no longer the attainment of perfect performance but rather the gift of a right relationship with God."[7]

Dealing with the Accuser

The ultimate weapon the Word of God gives us to heal a defective conscience and defend against condemnation is the blood of Christ. In Revelation 12:10-11 John tells us that the Accuser (Satan) accuses us day and night. His continual accusations affect us primarily through our consciences. John goes on to say that we defeat the Devil's accusations "by the blood of the Lamb." In Scripture blood always refers to death—usually violent death. Thus "the blood of the Lamb" in Revelation 12:11 refers to the violent death of Christ on the cross. And so it is by a proper understanding of the death of Jesus that we neutralize the accusations of Satan and spiritual abusers.

In Colossians 2:12-15 Paul shows how this is so:

[You have] been buried with him in baptism and raised with him through your faith in the power of God, who raised him from the dead.

When you were dead in your sins and in the uncircumcision of your sinful nature, God made you alive with Christ. He forgave us all our sins, having canceled the written code, with its regulations, that was against us and that stood opposed to us; he took it away, nailing it to the cross. And having disarmed the powers and authorities, he made a public spectacle of them, triumphing over them by the cross.

Here Paul states flatly that we are twice removed from the accusation of sin by the violent death of Jesus. First of all, our sins are forgiven (v. 13). And then the very basis for defining our sin is destroyed (v. 14): the written code with its regulations which stood against us has been nailed to the cross by Jesus. Not only are our sins blotted out, but even the means of describing them is gone forever. Now Satan the Accuser has no basis for accusation—no law to hold against us, and therefore no crime to accuse us of. This is how he has been disarmed (v. 15).

The tragedy, then, is that church leaders who preach the law as a means of manipulation and control actually rearm the devil in his work of accusation. What Jesus accomplished on the cross is effectively reversed by religious legalism. Or, as Paul explains in Galatians 4, when we come back under religious law, we actually come back under the demonic influences we were once rescued from.

So what are the practical steps we need to take to defend ourselves? Exactly how do we stop the Accuser's manipulation of our conscience through the death of Christ? When we do wrong (or think we do wrong), our conscience condemns us and demands some form of payment or punishment. Our instinctive response is to try to buy off our conscience, to punish ourselves or to let others punish us. If we truly have done wrong, the proper response is to repent, ask forgiveness from the Lord and anyone else we have hurt, and make restitution where appropriate. But when it comes to the nagging, nonspecific guilt and shame that are manipulated by Satan and spiritual abusers, we must respond with a specific, thoughtful application of Christ's blood to our conscience.

Satan and his ecclesiastical agents attempt to keep us from putting faith in Christ's blood. Instead they try to get us focused on our own efforts as the cure for a bad conscience. The ninth and tenth chapters of Hebrews make clear that all such human effort is utterly useless. "Gifts and sacrifice being offered were not able to clear the conscience of the worshiper" (Heb 9:9). No amount of submitting to authority, dying to self, praying to God or giving to an organization will clear a guilty or shamed conscience. All these works are vain attempts to get even with our conscience and are what the writer to the Hebrews appropriately terms "dead works."

Instead of dead religious works, we are to put faith in the blood of Christ, "who through the eternal Spirit offered himself without spot to God," to cleanse our conscience from "dead works" (Heb 9:14 KJV).

Religious performance cannot assuage guilt, because no amount of self-effort can ever atone for sin. If self-effort had worked, "the worshipers would have been cleansed once and for all, and would no longer have felt guilty for their sins" (Heb 10:2). Instead, religious self-help actually reinforces our guilt feelings. "Those sacrifices are an annual reminder of sins, because it is impossible for the blood of bulls and goats to take away sins" (Heb 10:3-4). Dead religious works promise freedom from guilt but instead remind us of it. The notion that our works can deliver us from shame and guilt is a lie. An old proverb says "lies have short legs"—that is, they will not carry us far and cannot long support us.

The writer to the Hebrews insists the only cure for guilt (real and imagined) and the shame that makes us vulnerable to spiritual abuse is the blood of Christ. So we are to turn from any and all religious performance as a means of becoming acceptable to God and others. Instead, "let us draw near to God with a sincere heart in full assurance of faith, having our hearts sprinkled to cleanse us from a guilty conscience" (Heb 10:22).

Paul says that he does not "set aside the grace of God, for if righteousness could be gained through the law, Christ died for nothing" (Gal 2:21). If we could atone for our sins through religious performance, then we would not need a Savior to shed his blood for us. But Jesus already has spilled his blood, so why should we continue to suffer for sins he suffered for?

In practical terms, this means that when the accusations of Satan or spiritual abusers stab our conscience, it is best not to argue. Rather, we must agree that we are sinners and do need to be punished. Then with full assurance of faith, we can show our conscience and our accusers the blood of the Lamb—the violent death of Jesus, who was punished for us already. Conscience demands payment for sin, and the good news is that payment is already and forever paid in full. As

Martin Luther once said, "You should not believe your conscience and your feelings more than the word which the Lord who receives sinners preaches to us."

What to Do Now

Reading this book, you may have concluded that your church has problems but is not abusive. The problems it faces are the result of social forces other than spiritual abuse.

Others of you have discovered that beyond a doubt, your church is significantly abusive. You must now decide whether you should stay and fight for change or leave.

Others are still wondering. Your church may show some symptoms of being an abusive group, but not all of them. It may have virtues that seem to compensate for its possible abuses.

To aid in assessing your church and deciding what you should do, let's briefly review the symptoms of abusive religion according to Jesus in Matthew 23:

1. Abusive leaders base their spiritual authority on their position or office rather than on their service to the group. Their style of leadership is authoritarian.

2. Leaders in abusive churches often say one thing but do another. Their words and deeds do not match.

3. They manipulate people by making them feel guilty for not measuring up spiritually. They lay heavy religious loads on people and make no effort to lift those loads. You know that you are in an abusive church if the loads just keep getting heavier.

4. Abusive leaders are preoccupied with looking good. They labor to keep up appearance. They stifle any criticism that puts them in a bad light.

5. They seek honorific titles and special privileges that elevate them above the group. They promote a class system with themselves at the top.

6. Their communication is not straight. Their speech becomes especially vague and confusing when they are defending themselves.

7. They major on minor issues to the neglect of the truly important ones. They are conscientious about religious details but neglect God's larger agendas.

If your church rates high on these negative indicators, it is significantly spiritually abusive. Now something must be done. You may choose to stay and fight for change. Bear in mind, however, that most abusive religious systems are very well rationalized and well defended. Abusive leaders are unlikely to respond well to your rational objections and constructive criticisms. Spiritual abuse is never the result of confused thinking. It is caused by a lust for power.

Leaving may be your only option. But it may not be easy.

One of the major indicators of an abusive system is the difficulty people face in leaving it. Jesus made it easy for people to leave him. The back door was always open. Leaders who truly follow Jesus also allow people to go when they choose to. Abusive leaders, on the other hand, erect significant obstacles to deserters.

In order to surmount these obstacles, ask yourself, "Didn't Jesus himself tell us not to trust the Pharisees and not to follow the blind guides?" Ask yourself if you can go on giving your time, energy and money to support something you now know is destructive. Can you go on placing your family at risk by continually exposing them to the toxins of spiritual abuse?

Sometimes the most loving thing we can do for abusive leaders is to leave them. Sometimes the most humane act is to let an abusive church die.

If you must leave an abusive church, you may go through a painful period of anger, depression, even despair. These are normal responses. Take time to take care of yourself. Resist the well-meaning exhortations of friends who tell you to "snap out of it" in Jesus' name. If you were hit by a bus, you would need time to recover. Something almost as serious as that has happened to you. Take time. Let yourself heal.

Finally, resist the temptation to stay away from church just because of a bad church experience. There actually are more good churches out there than bad ones. Find a church where you can safely tell your story and find healing. Never give up on the church. God doesn't.

The Fire Has Passed

When I was five years old, my grandfather and I stood in the middle of a 120-acre wheat field that was dry and ready for harvest. He said that if ever I happened to be there when the field caught fire (which it did occasionally), I should not run. A wind-swept blaze travels faster than anyone can run. Instead, I should immediately start a fire right where I stood, then stand in the midst of the burned-down stubble so that the larger blaze could not reach me. He said, "Fire cannot pass where fire has already passed."

The fire of God's judgment, the terrible punishment for sin, has already passed through Christ. Now those who are standing in Christ have no judgment or condemnation to fear: because fire cannot pass where fire has already passed.

As we arm ourselves with this gospel and hold firm to this faith, we can delight in a clear conscience. In time, the accusations of the devil and of spiritual abusers will lose their manipulative power over us. And we are free to learn how to live with spontaneity and a light heart.

In turn this freedom will lead to another freedom, freedom from bitterness toward those who have abused us in the past. The deep sense of our radical freedom and forgiveness liberates us to freely forgive all others.

The burdens of bitterness destroy peace, joy, freedom and life itself. Bitterness cripples, enslaves and renders us useless for the kingdom of God. This is the design of the enemy; this may be the prime reason he promotes spiritual abuse. Many people have been rendered useless by bitterness resulting from abuse, but forgiveness opens the way back to spiritual vitality.

Jesus came not only to lift the burdens of ecclesiastical abuse off our shoulders but also to deliver us from the crippling burdens of bitterness. Jesus forgave perfectly, and his power to forgive actually resides within us. It may be very hard to forgive those who have wronged us, but Jesus' power is with us in the struggle.

The will to power exists within every person, but in the Christian it is converted into the will to serve.
Donald Bloesch

Two cities have been formed by two loves: ... in the one the princes and the nations it subdues are ruled by the love of ruling; in the other, the princes and subjects serve one another in love.
St. Augustine

You know that the rulers of the Gentiles lord it over them, and their high officials exercise authority over them. Not so with you. Instead, whoever wants to become great among you must be your servant.
Jesus Christ

Not that we lord it over your faith, but we work with you for your joy.
The apostle Paul

9

HEALTHY CHURCH LEADERSHIP

*I*n the early chapters of this book we learned from Jesus to identify and reject spiritual abuse. And this can help us recognize good leadership when we see it. If we turn Jesus' negative comments about abusive leaders into positive statements, we have a start on defining leadership that is healthy and nonabusive.

Abusive leaders, according to Jesus, take for themselves authority and power based on position and office (Mt 23:2, 7). By contrast, healthy leaders shun honorific titles and are effective in caring for the needs of God's people. It is by servant leadership that the nonabusive leader exercises influence.

Abusive leaders oppress and manipulate men and women by tying up heavy loads and laying them on their shoulders (Mt 23:4). They

multiply rules and regulations to induce guilt and shame in their
followers in order to control them. Nonabusive leaders lift those
burdens off, directing their followers to Jesus Christ for rest and for
"yokes" that are light and fit well (Mt 11:28-30).

Abusive leaders do everything for show (Mt 23:5). They take exalted
titles, demand special privileges and insist on playing by different
rules (Mt 23:6-7). They flaunt external symbols of spirituality, but on
the inside they are spiritually dead. They use words deceitfully for
self-promotion. It is more important for them to look and sound like
men and women of God than to actually be men and women of God
(Mt 23:16-22). Healthy leaders, by contrast, spend no time or energy
on their image. They live simply and transparently before people.
They say what they mean and mean what they say (Mt 5:37).

Abusive leaders invert spiritual values; they major on minor issues
while minimizing people's significant needs. They are scrupulous religious performers while neglecting justice and mercy (Mt 23:23-24).
Nonabusive leaders, on the other hand, stand ready to jettison religious protocol when it conflicts with real human need. They major on
majors (Mt 12:9-13).

Abusive leaders slam the door of the kingdom of God in the faces
of men and women (Mt 23:13) by denying the full messianic ministry
of Jesus or by teaching that it costs something to get. In contrast,
healthy leaders swing wide the doors of the kingdom of God, proclaiming that it is all free to us by grace through faith in the King.

Those who cultivate abusive leadership styles often do so out of
deep personal need. Most authoritarians are fearful and insecure.
Since they feel threatened, they seek to create safe environments for
themselves by maintaining control over others. By contrast, healthy
leaders know God's free forgiveness and lavish acceptance through
Christ and so are able to love, accept and serve others from that
position of strength.

Some abusive leaders use people in their quest for personal heroics, because their goal in life is to become someone great. Nonabusive leaders make obedience to God and meeting other people's legitimate needs their aim in life. If heroism is required in the course of service, a true leader is up to this by the power of God. But any prominence gained through heroic service is incidental.

So examining the negative characteristics of abusive leaders has given us a start on identifying the positive attributes of healthy leaders. Now let's take a broader look at New Testament teachings on leadership.

New Testament Leadership

Many of us who debate the structure and function of church government are surprised when we read what the New Testament actually teaches on this subject. The New Testament writers seem oddly relaxed regarding church government and leadership. Unlike us, they appear to have little interest in determining who is in charge and how decisions are made. What is mentioned on these subjects is so ambiguous that earnest Bible students draw radically conflicting conclusions from the texts. Such diverse groups as Roman Catholic, Plymouth Brethren, Anglican, Baptist, Presbyterian and Pentecostal all look to the same New Testament passages in support of their opposing ecclesiastical structures. This should cause us to pause before asserting what the Bible "clearly teaches" regarding church order and leadership.

The government and leadership structures of the early church may not have been rigidly defined and standardized. One thing is clear, however, and that is that the church during the New Testament era rejected hierarchy as its basic governmental structure. In Matthew 20:25 Jesus told his followers, "The rulers of the Gentiles lord it *over* them." That is to say, the world structures its institutions hierarchically, with those who rule dominating those who are ruled. He went on to say, "Not so with you. Instead, whoever wants to become great *among* you must be your servant" (v. 26). That is to say, it is good to desire greatness, but in the church, greatness is the reward of effective servanthood.

Jesus himself was a spiritual leader with his own group of followers. He was among them as one who served. He washed their feet. He laid down his life for them. Jesus' teaching and example of servant leadership were revolutionary. The leader served his followers! No other religious or political figure in history had ever done that.

The book of Acts and the Epistles reveal that the early church enacted Jesus' egalitarian ideal. In the New Testament church, leaders were among the people and serving them. Over the years, however, the primitive church gradually fell back into the hierarchical structures that Jesus had condemned. In time, the old way of ruling over the people again became the norm.

Ecclesiastical hierarchies (then and now) are founded on a sharp distinction between clergy and laity. The professional ministry (clergy) exists apart from the people (laity). The clergy play by different rules. They have different privileges, answer to a different set of expectations and are judged by different standards of conduct.

The clergy are thought of as having privileged access to God's higher wisdom. While spiritual leaders protest such assumptions, their unspoken signals often contradict their words. The laity may indeed conduct activities labeled "ministry." But the real "ministry" is often ferociously defended and jealously guarded.

This difference gives leaders the high ground in ecclesiastical hierarchies and automatically affords them the power to manipulate and control those beneath them. The clergy-laity distinction is essential to the construction of hierarchies which often become abusive.

A friend who knew that I was writing on spiritual abuse sent me a copy of the constitution of a Midwestern church. Under the heading "Principles of Church Order" I read, "The relationship of Pastor-members is not one of equality but of authority. The Pastor rules over the members just as a shepherd rules over his sheep, a father over his children and a king over his citizens."

If this distinction between leader and led were dissolved, it would help clean up the environment in which spiritual abuse thrives. The right and most effective way of doing this is simply to read the New Testament and let the text speak for itself. It becomes apparent that there was no hierarchy of any kind in the early church.

Equality in the Spirit

The absence of hierarchical structures in the New Testament church is a radical departure not only from the world but also from the way God's people were organized in the Old Testament. Under the Old Covenant, the people of God were structured in a hierarchy with elite male leadership at the top (prophet, priest, king and the like). These leaders existed apart from the people with their own set of rules, privileges and expectations. The defining mark of these prophet-priest-king leaders was the anointing of the Holy Spirit. In fact, most Old Testament saints did not have the Holy Spirit. The Spirit was given only to a very few elder male leaders. So in Old Testament times, this privileged relationship with the Holy Spirit set leaders apart from the people.

On the Day of Pentecost, the Old Covenant (clergy-laity) distinction dissolved as the Holy Spirit was poured out on all of God's people. The event had been predicted in Joel 2:28-29, and Peter recognized that the Pentecost outpouring was the fulfillment of Joel's prophecy:

In the last days, God says,

I will pour out my Spirit on all people.

Your sons and daughters will prophesy,

your young men will see visions,

your old men will dream dreams.

Even on my servants, both men and women,

I will pour out my Spirit in those days,

and they will prophesy. (Acts 2:17-18)

In the Old Covenant it was only the Spirit-anointed prophets who could prophesy, but under the New Covenant the prophet-people distinction has disappeared. Now, since God's people all have the Holy Spirit, all are expected to prophesy.

This community experience of the Holy Spirit means that other distinctions on which hierarchies are built also disappear. Not only the old will lead, but also the young. Not just the Jew will speak for God, but also the Gentile. Not only men will minister, but women as well. This is the background for Paul's radically antihierarchical statement in Galatians 3:28: "There is neither Jew nor Greek, slave nor free, male nor female, for you are all one in Christ Jesus." The previous hierarchical structure has been destroyed, and all Christians are made one by the one Spirit we have each received (Eph 4:4-5).

In the New Covenant, leadership offices are not inherited, nor are they awarded to members of a specific class. Ministry function is no longer hierarchical but charismatic (gift-based). The Holy Spirit of the New Covenant is the Spirit of Joel's prophecy, who assigns ministry and leadership functions to whomever he chooses. The Spirit is unconscious of age, race, sex or rank. He gives gifts to whom he will for the common good (1 Cor 12:7-11). Now leadership roles do not denote a special class but rather a particular mode of service. Therefore leaders "labor *among* you," as Paul habitually says.

The lack of hierarchical leaders in the local churches that Paul founded is demonstrated by how he constructs his church letters. First of all, Paul does not address the leaders but writes directly to the church as a whole. When he wants to correct some worship practice, he addresses not the worship leader but the church. When he expresses concern over a pastoral issue, he confronts not the pastors but the people. When he deals with an administrative concern, he directs his words not to the administrators but to the whole congregation. Paul never singles out a clergy class, holding them accountable for church affairs, nor does he make them responsible for carrying out his apostolic directives.

When Paul speaks of specialized spiritual gifts within the body (which includes leadership gifts), he demands absolute parity between them (1 Cor 12:12-26). When he refers specifically to those gifted in leadership, such as apostles and prophets, he speaks of them as servants among the people (Eph 4:11-13) rather than rulers over them.

Discipline Without Hierarchy

The language of hierarchy is conspicuously absent from the New Testament, even where one might logically expect to find it. If ever there were a time for the clergy class to step forward and take charge, it would be when discipline of serious sin is called for. Yet the New Testament always presents church discipline as a community rather than a leadership function.

The Magna Carta of church discipline is Matthew 18:15-18. It begins, "If your brother sins against you, go and show him his fault." The person in the church with the authority and responsibility to initiate discipline is the one who first observes the sin. Jesus makes clear that church discipline is not the responsibility of leadership but rather the duty of the people of God as a whole. We disobey him and perpetuate a false clergy-laity distinction when we refer disciplinary concerns to leaders.[1]

Like Jesus, Paul also sees church discipline as a church rather than a leadership function. When he confronts flagrant sin on two occasions in the Corinthian church (1 Cor 5:1-13; 6:1-11), he speaks to the people as a whole rather than to the sinners or to the leaders. He does not go after the offenders in his apostolic capacity, nor does he instruct the leaders to do so in theirs. Rather, he turns his guns on the whole church for its failure to deal with these matters. In 5:1-13 the man in sin is not mentioned, nor is his partner. The whole people of

God have failed, and it is *their* failure that concerns Paul most. In 6:1-11 Paul counsels the defendant and the plaintiff only after scolding the entire church for allowing such a thing to happen in the first place. So in all the New Testament teaching on church discipline, leaders are never given responsibility that is different from or higher than the responsibility of the rest of the people.

The New Testament does not present any specific governmental structure as ultimately authoritative. It's clear, though, that no clergy-laity distinction exists in the early church and that none was ever intended. As Gordon Fee sums it up, "Leadership in the New Testament is never seen as outside or above the people themselves, but simply as part of the whole, essential to its well-being but governed by the same set of rules. They are not set apart by 'ordination'; rather their gifts are part of the Spirit's work among the whole people."[2]

The style of leadership exemplified by Jesus and his followers is based on and motivated by servanthood. Its purpose is nothing less than reproduction of Jesus' character and ministry skills in all the church. The reward of such leadership is freedom and joy for both leaders and followers.

But there is an important caveat to make here. All members of the body of Christ are equal, but that does not make us all the same. God-given gifts set some people apart for special service to the community. Someone called to be a medical doctor is different from others by virtue of special education and training. In much the same way, someone called to the public ministry is different from others by virtue of special education and training. That training does not elevate the minister, however, but rather calls him or her to a more skilled and effective service. The apostle Peter directs public ministers to "be shepherds of God's flock that is under your care, serving . . . not lording it over those entrusted to you, but being examples to the flock" (1 Pet 5:2-3).

Servant Power

When I present my views on servant leadership at conferences and seminars, the pastors in the group often ask: "How can a 'servant leader' at the same time be a *strong* leader?" Pastors appear to be especially concerned about leadership's relationship to authority and power. In fact, the public ministry seems to have attracted an inordinate number of insecure men who want to see themselves as leaders, as those in charge.

Cheryl Forbes remarks on how CTi (Christianity Today Inc.) cashed in on clergy's preoccupation with issues of power and leadership with the publication of its magazine for clergy, *Leadership*. She reminds us that the theme of the first issue was "Power and Authority." In introducing it, the publishers asked, " 'Who runs the church?' 'Who should have the authority and power?' . . . The editors assume that power is something that ministers must have."[3]

Forbes says the editors of that first issue missed the central point of true Christian leadership: "The first issue of *Leadership* may offer pragmatic help for the minister to maneuver and manipulate his way to control, but it offers little theological guidance as to the nature and role of a true leader. Jesus, the servant leader, cannot be found."[4]

I distinctly recall reading that first issue of *Leadership* and how it initially appealed to me for all the wrong reasons. As a youthful, insecure pastor of a large congregation, I believed the advice I most needed had to do with how I could gain control in order to accomplish what I was called to accomplish.

Of course church leaders need power to function. I now understand, however, that they gain authority not by succeeding at power games but by succeeding as servants. This principle applies not just in the body of Christ but also in the world. Power and influence are given to those who serve or appear to serve. Serve people well and in time they will usually grant you authority. George Grant recognizes the operation of this principle even in some functions of government:

"There is a fundamental principle of dominion ... through service. This principle is understood by the modern welfare state. The politicians and planners recognize that the agency that supplies charity in the name of the people will gain the allegiance of the people. So they 'serve' and so they gain dominion."[5]

Even secular institutions have discovered power through service. While it may be perverted by some, God has built this principle into the structure of creation. Servanthood is the God-ordained path to power and influence. Jesus Christ, the greatest servant of all, led the way.

> Jesus said to them, "The kings of the Gentiles lord it over them.
> ... But you are not to be like that. Instead, the greatest among you
> should be like the youngest, and the one who rules like the one who
> serves.... I am among you as one who serves." (Lk 22:25-27)

The question "How can servants also be strong leaders?" displays ignorance not only of the Bible and social forces but also of church history. The greatest leaders down through the church age did not depend on hierarchical or institutional power but on the voluntary support of their followers. When leaders serve faithfully and effectively, people grant them more and more freedom to lead. Most people understand that if someone is dedicated to building them up and solving their problems, that person can be trusted with power. True servants diffuse any fear of their leadership.

This dynamic should also work in reverse, so that when leaders begin to abuse the power entrusted to them, followers withdraw that power. This kind of accountability of leaders to followers not only protects the people from spiritual abuse but also delivers an effective wake-up call to budding spiritual abusers.

Accountability initiated by the congregation also serves as a kind of preventive medicine. If a congregation makes clear at the outset that the only power it allows leaders is the power to serve, those with a conflicting agenda will look elsewhere. When the only authority offered to a leader is the authority to build others up, those wanting authoritarian power are repelled.

Leadership Styles

While a true leader uses his or her power to serve others, this does not imply a fixed style of leadership. An important component of a servant's heart is flexibility in dealing with the variety of human needs he or she is faced with. A servant leader may act nondirectively with one person and exactly the opposite with another. A true leader may help one group reach a consensus while he or she functions almost as an autocrat in other groups. People's needs and level of maturity must determine how the servant leader serves them.

This needs to be made clear, given my previous negative comments regarding authoritarian leadership. Authoritarian leadership is not evil in every situation. New Christians, like beginners in anything, need authorities to provide structure and give direction.

Years ago, when I directed an inner-city mission serving young drug and alcohol offenders, I found it both loving and necessary to set firm boundaries at first. These kids converted off the streets had no structure in their lives and possessed no self-discipline, no sense of time, no personal boundaries. Conversion did not make them mature adults. They needed strong, directive parenting, and love demanded that I and other mature believers provide it for them. But soon those who wanted to grow and mature did so. After that happened I became less directive, encouraging more and more freedom (often more than they wanted). In time they became functional adults, and some even took up leadership responsibilities alongside me.

A servant leader becomes strongly directive when love demands it. When necessary he or she can step in and take control of a dangerous situation. But as followers begin to function responsibly, the previous parent-child relationship evolves into a friendship between peers.

Jesus himself recognized that different people are at different levels of maturity. To one he said, "Go and sin no more." To others he said, "Go into all the world and make disciples." He once described the "faithful and wise servant" as the one who prepares food for other members of the household. To one person that wise and faithful servant will serve milk, to another he or she will serve meat.

The consistency of a servant leader is not in a fixed style of leadership, but in a commitment to meet people where they are and assist them on to maturity. And the result of such leadership is joy for both follower and leader.

The Fruit of Servanthood

When the apostle Paul sums up the burden of his own pastoral ministry, he says to the church at Corinth, "Not that we lord it over your faith, but we work with you for your joy" (2 Cor 1:24). In those few words he gives the essential aim of servant leadership.

I find it very interesting that he begins with a deterrent to ecclesiastical abuse. Before he states the positive purpose of his leadership, he cautions against the wrong kind of leadership: "not that we lord it over your faith." As I have said already, Paul was the most apostolic-minded of all the apostles, yet he never pulled rank on his followers. He never positioned himself as lord over his converts—even though he often took issue with them over concerns that he felt passionately about. Rather than demand submission from his followers, he argued the truth of his case. Rather than assert his authority, he persuaded them to agree with him. Winning his point depended on the power of his case, not the power of his position.

If Paul was not lord over his churches, what then was he? In 2 Corinthians 1:24 he essentially describes himself as a helper. The New International Version translates the word for "helper" (*synergos*) as "we work with you." This humble self-designation sums up Paul's function as leader. He casts himself as one who works with the Corinthians in a servant role rather than one who stands above them in a ruler role. He emphasizes his function as servant rather than his office as apostle.

Paul then tells the Corinthians the overall purpose of his servant leadership: "we work with you for your joy." Imagine, the greatest missionary evangelist of the New Testament era (and of all time) sees his first responsibility to his converts as promoting not their faith, holiness or obedience but their joy!

We should keep in mind that he is writing to the troublesome and contentious Corinthians. In the course of his letter he *will* encourage their holiness and obedience, as well as challenge their financial giving, but he always maintains that being a good Christian is first of all knowing and loving God. And we come to God not because we are bludgeoned into it but because we are attracted by his mercy and grace as well as his own joy in us. Thomas Smith sheds light on Paul's priority of promoting joy among his followers: "The man who understands the dynamics of Christian faith and life will realize that what God wants from his people is, first and last, their hearts. He is interested in them and wants them to be interested in him, for himself. Joy is inextricably bound up, therefore, with faith in Christ and love to Christ."[6]

To put it more simply, to come to God is to come to joy.

This may sound odd to some Christian leaders, but it shouldn't. After all, to know God is to experience joy. Psalm 43:4 says, "I will go . . . to God, my joy and my delight." The writer of Psalm 16:11 tells God, "You will fill me with joy in your presence, with eternal pleasures at your right hand." Karl Barth insists that this is the goal of theological study as well: "Evangelical theology is concerned with Immanuel, God with us! Having this God for its object, it can be nothing else but the most thankful and happy science."[7] To come to God is to come to joy.

Furthermore, the Christian disciplines bring joy. There is joy in Bible reading. "The precepts of the LORD are right, giving joy to the heart" (Ps 19:8). There is joy in prayer. When Jesus instructs us to pray, he says, "Until now you have not asked for anything in my name. Ask and you will receive, and your joy will be complete" (Jn 16:24). There is joy in Christian leadership. When the apostle John confesses his own motive for serving his followers, he says, "We write this to make our joy complete" (1 Jn 1:4).

At the end of the day, the reward for having served God and his people well is joy. When Paul discusses with the Thessalonians his own reward for laboring among them, he asks, "For what is our hope, our joy? . . . Is it not you?" He then assures them, "Indeed, you are our glory and our joy" (1 Thess 2:19-20). To be converted to Christ is to be converted to joy. Joy is at the heart of the Christian experience, and joy is the leader's reward for promoting it in others.

When the writers of the old creed stated that "the chief end of man [and woman] is to glorify God and enjoy him forever," they were not talking about two separate things. As John Piper notes, "They said 'chief end,' not 'chief ends.' Glorifying God and enjoying him forever were one end in their minds."[8] If the chief end of Christians is to enjoy God, it should be easy to agree with Paul that the chief end of Christian leadership is to promote that enjoyment.

Paul establishes this same point negatively in his letter to the Galatians. The grace-killing religious legalists and spiritual abusers in Galatia had tied up heavy religious loads and laid them on the shoulders of Paul's converts, destroying their joy. Paul asks them, "What has happened to all your joy?" (Gal 4:15). Satanically inspired spiritual abuse comes in all shapes and sizes, but it always attacks joy. Piper may be right when he asserts that "Satan's number one objective is to destroy our joy of faith."[9]

Joy is finally one of the fruits by which people of faith are recognized, according to Jesus. Healthy leaders will know joy and will promote it in their followers.

*Church discipline arises out of the gospel itself. The aim of
the gospel is reconciliation, the reconciliation
wrought by Christ and offered to sinners.*
John White and Ken Blue

*If your brother sins against you, go and show him his fault,
just between the two of you. If he listens to you,
you have won your brother over.*
Jesus Christ

10
HEALTHY CHURCH DISCIPLINE

*M*any people see church discipline as a traditional tool of spiritual abuse. In their experience, "discipline" has been invoked by leaders to control and punish their followers. So the very phrase *healthy church discipline* seems to them an oxymoron—a contradiction in terms.

Years ago I made a comprehensive study of church discipline over the past two thousand years.[1] A primary question I wanted to answer was why church discipline has fallen into disuse among churches in the West.[2] My investigation suggested that the primary reason is that church discipline in the past often became so cruel, destructive and counterproductive that much of the church reacted by discontinuing it altogether.

But the proper response to bad church discipline is not no church discipline but good church discipline. As Geddess MacGregor puts it, "To abandon discipline because it has been ill administered is as unwarranted as it would be to abolish worship on the grounds that it has been ill conducted."[3]

Past Abuses
If we are to restore healthy, nonabusive church discipline, we need first to understand what went wrong in the past. The tendency toward abusiveness in this realm usually begins when the goal of church discipline is defined too narrowly. Historically, the primary goal of church discipline was the purification of the congregation. Speaking for many in and beyond his own tradition, John Calvin states that the leading purposes for discipline are (1) that those who lead a filthy and infamous life must not be called Christian and not profane the Lord's Supper and (2) that the good not be corrupted by the company of the wicked.[4]

That is to say, church discipline is for upholding the corporate purity of the church and for halting the moral corruption of its members. The modern theologian G. C. Berkouwer echoes the church's historical view that discipline is primarily to promote purity in the congregation: "When sins come into view which defile the sanctuary and profane God's holy name, the admonition follows: 'Consecrate yourselves therefore and be holy; for I am the LORD your God. . . .' New Testament discipline is most closely connected to the church's holiness."[5]

The history of church discipline shows us that a singular concern for corporate and personal holiness has led leaders to take drastic and even cruel measures with those judged to be impure. In some extreme cases, the impure person was removed from the church by execution. The Spanish Inquisition is one example.

While Scripture makes a connection between congregational holiness and church discipline (1 Cor 5:1-13), it also teaches that there are other motives that ought to take precedence. These are (1) calling the offender back to true Christian discipleship and (2) restoring personal relationships that have been violated by sin (Mt 18:15-18).[6] If our goal in church discipline is first to restore the offender's relationship to Christ and the church, we will of necessity treat him or her with care and respect.

Though church discipline has not been widely practiced in Western churches in the past century, in recent years it has been making a strong comeback. Unfortunately, some churches have not learned from history. They are once again seizing upon the idea of church discipline simply as a means of controlling the behavior of their followers.

Abusive Discipline: An Example

A friend of mine recently gave me a chilling account of how church discipline was conducted within the congregation he formerly attended. This church was conservative and doctrinally orthodox. No one who read its statement of faith would suspect that there was anything amiss. But the pastor of this group of 150 people was authoritarian and dictatorial. He gathered around him a small group of supporters who fortified him and shared in his power. The pastor and these assistant leaders used what they called "corrective church discipline" to keep the rest of the members in line. When they spotted someone stepping out of line (that is, deviating from the church's doctrinal beliefs or its detailed code of behavior), these leaders as a group would initiate "corrective discipline."

As the first step in the disciplinary procedure, the pastor and at least one other leader would pay a visit to the alleged offender's home. The pastor and his assistant(s) would explain what was wrong with the person and demand change. The accused was expected to fully agree with the leaders and then promise to make the prescribed changes quickly. If there was not total agreement about the alleged sin or the required changes, or if the accused did not exhibit a "submissive spirit" in the process, the second stage of discipline was then imposed.

This second stage consisted of an announcement to the entire church that the accused was "under discipline." The offender was barred from the Lord's Table and from all church gatherings except the Sunday-morning public meeting. All members of the congregation were expected to limit contact with the accused. If the person was part of a church ministry, he or she was immediately removed from it. The offender remained "under discipline" until the pastor and his supporters lifted the disciplinary sanctions.

After an unspecified period of virtual ostracism, the pastor and his supporters determined whether the disciplinary measures were producing the desired effects. If not, the disciplined person was then charged with committing the sin of "contumacy"—that is, "the crime of holding authority in contempt." This sin was punishable by excommunication.

Excommunication was carried out at a congregational meeting called for that purpose. The accused was asked to attend, but rarely did. The pastor and his supporters stood at the front of the meeting hall facing the congregation. In front of them stood a table that held many lit candles.

Following a public rehearsal of the offender's sin and an account of the leaders' efforts to correct the sinner, the pastor picked up one of the candles and turned it over, snuffing it out. He then said, "We hand you over to Satan for the destruction of the flesh."

My friend was present at one of these meetings. He said the fear it produced in him and in others was profound. "You only had to see it once to know you never wanted it to happen to you," he told me. "The fear made you quickly fall into line with the wishes of the leaders."

This church violated Scripture at every turn, as we shall see in a moment. So it should not surprise us that the results were evil. This example is helpful in our study, however, because we can contrast this abusive procedure with what the Bible teaches and so see more clearly what healthy church discipline looks like.

Jesus' Guidelines for Discipline

The primary text to guide church discipline is Jesus' teaching on the subject in Matthew 18:15-18.

> If your brother sins ... go and show him his fault, just between the two of you. If he listens to you, you have won your brother over. But if he will not listen, take one or two others along, so that 'every matter may be established by the testimony of two or three witnesses'. If he refuses to listen to them, tell it to the church; and if he refuses to listen even to the church, treat him as you would a pagan or a tax collector.

The church my friend described went wrong at the start by viewing discipline as a top-down, leader-initiated procedure. The leaders took sole responsibility for deciding who was to be disciplined and when. This error is often what sets abusive church discipline in motion.

By contrast, Jesus says that church discipline is the responsibility of all, not just the leaders. The person who first needs to approach a suspected offender is the one who first observes the sin. "If you see your brother sinning, go and show him his fault." There is no hint here that discipline is a matter between superior and inferior, leader and led. It is rather to occur among brothers and sisters.

The second error committed in our example of abusive church discipline is that the first disciplinary approach was made by the pastor and at least one coleader. Jesus says clearly that the first approach is to be made in private—"just between the two of you." The reason for this initial privacy is to guard against the sin's becoming public knowledge, which would promote gossip and unnecessary hurt.

In our abusive example, the prime motive for discipline was to correct and, if needed, punish the follower who had deviated from the church's ideological or behavioral norms. If necessary, the deviant would be removed to prevent the spread of contamination. Jesus' teaching reveals radically different concerns.

To begin with, Matthew 18:15-17 comes just after the story of a shepherd going after a sheep who had strayed (vv. 10-14). The brother who has supposedly sinned is regarded as a sheep who has wandered away from the fellowship. The person who first becomes aware of this is to act as a good shepherd, trying to bring the wanderer back. The motive for the first disciplinary approach is not to push the contamination out of the church, but to draw the lost sheep back into it. The prime concern is the person, not the sin. As Jesus says, "If he listens to you [responds positively to your first disciplinary approach], you have won your brother over." Sin stresses and damages fellowship. Successfully confronting sin removes this stress and promotes reconciliation.

In our example of abusive church discipline, the leaders moved from the first confrontation straight to a public announcement and then on to excommunication proper. In Jesus' teaching, the first, private attempt at reconciliation with the wandering sheep is to be followed up by at least one subsequent meeting for the same purpose: reconciliation. "But if he will not listen to you, take one or two others along" (v. 16). If the first meeting does not result in restored fellowship, a second meeting with one or two others may be effective.

Everything I said earlier about the motive and spirit of the one-to-one meeting applies to this second, small group meeting. Adding one or two people to this second attempt at reconciliation provides added discernment. It may be that the person who initiated the discipline actually overreacted or misjudged the other. The one or two counselors can assess this. If it turns out that the alleged sinner really should repent of some attitude or behavior, the counselors add their persuasion to the first person's concerns. But even at this level the issue needs to be contained within the smallest circle possible, so as to protect against unnecessary wear and tear on relationships within the larger church body. These private and semiprivate meetings are not the preliminaries to excommunication; their purpose is to make excommunication unnecessary.

Finally, "if he refuses to listen to them, tell it to the church" (v. 17). If all the previous steps have been handled properly, this final stage is rarely needed; in a few cases, however, we may have to take the problem to the church. When we do that, it looks nothing like the excommunication service in my friend's story of the abusive church. That excommunication service was set up to excommunicate. In Matthew 18:17 the church service is the church body's coming together to add its collective weight to the task of "winning the brother" back into fellowship. It is the flock's last-ditch attempt to bring a wanderer back in.

It is not the responsibility nor the prerogative of the leaders to administer this final stage of discipline. This final act belongs to the church as a whole, just as the first several stages belong to the church as a whole. Commenting on Matthew 18, Hans Küng states: "It is the whole church, the whole community of disciples, which bears the authority to forgive. . . . Final judgments, particularly negative ones, are the responsibility of the community."[7]

If the community should fail to reconcile the sinner to itself and the lost sheep insists on remaining lost, then the church will "treat him as you would a pagan or a tax collector" (v. 17). In our abusive church's example, this meant handing the person over to Satan and acting as if he or she no longer existed. This could hardly be what Jesus intended. We know this by the way *he* treated publicans and tax collectors. He did not treat them as dead, nor did he hand them over to the devil. He pursued them, engaged them in conversation and kept on calling them to follow him (Mt 9:9). He did not welcome them as true disciples without true repentance and faith. But he kept talking to them in hopes that they would repent and believe.

If the church is to follow Jesus, our church discipline will have teeth. In the end there will be a formal break in fellowship patterns for unrepentant sinners. But we will remain open to their return. The parable of the return of the prodigal son may be Jesus' clearest expression of the attitude and hope we should have for an errant brother or sister.

> Corrective church discipline begins with the recognition that sin produces alienation. It devotes itself to overcoming that alienation. But if it fails in its objective, the church, like the father in the story of the prodigal son, never ceases to long for and to wait for the return of the prodigal. And when the prodigal returns its delight knows no bounds.[8]

If we follow Christ's clear teaching on church discipline, we will be effective in saving lost sheep from destruction and equally effective in solving relational problems. And abusive discipline will not be a problem in our churches. Finally, the Bible's message to spiritual abusers and their victims is, Follow Jesus. Come home to the father. God awaits you with open arms.

Notes

Chapter 1: An Invitation to Freedom

[1]Ezekiel 37, for instance, is an ancient account of how religious authorities sinned against their followers. It reveals the plight of those who get injured, frightened and lost under the "care" of false shepherds.

[2]I first saw the term *spiritual abuse* in print in a book by David Johnson and Jeff VanVonderen, *The Subtle Power of Spiritual Abuse* (Minneapolis: Bethany House, 1991).

[3]Ronald Enroth, *Churches That Abuse* (Grand Rapids: Zondervan, 1992), p. 29.

[4]Satanic ritual abuse is beyond the scope of this book, as are the specific problems surrounding sexual abuse by clergy.

[5]Most names have been changed, and one illustration is a composite of two people. Otherwise the stories I use are recorded as they were reported to me.

[6]Juanita and Dale Ryan, *Recovering from Spiritual Abuse* (Downers Grove, Ill.: Inter-Varsity Press, 1992), p. 9.

[7]For a history of this movement and an insider's view of its problems, see Ron and Vicky Berk's *Damaged Disciples* (Grand Rapids, Mich.: Zondervan, 1992).

[8]Ibid., p. 86.

Chapter 2: The Seat of Moses—The Power to Abuse

[1]Jesus referred to himself as the living bread who gives life (Jn 6:35, 51-58) and as the source of living water (Jn 4:10; 7:37-38). He also said, "I am . . . the life" (Jn 11:25; 14:6).

[2]F. Dale Brunner, *Matthew,* Word Biblical Commentary (Dallas: Word Books, 1990), 2:808.

[3]C. S. Lewis, *Reflections on the Psalms* (New York: Harcourt Brace, 1958), pp. 31-32.

[4]David Seamands, *Putting Away Childish Things* (Wheaton, Ill.: Victor Books, 1982), p. 46.

[5]David Hill, *The Gospel of Matthew* (London: Oliphants, 1977), p. 310.

[6]Anthony Saldarini, *Pharisees, Scribes and Sadducees In Palestinian Society* (Wilmington, Del.: Michael Glazier, 1988), p. 111.

[7]Watchman Nee, *The Body of Christ* (New York: Christian Fellowship Publishers, 1978), pp. 20-21.

[8]Watchman Nee, *Spiritual Authority* (New York: Christian Fellowship Publishers, 1972), p. 71.

[9]Derek Prince, *Discipleship, Shepherding, Commitment* (n.p.: Derek Prince Publishers), p. 18.

[10]Attributed to "the Boston Movement"; quoted in Ronald Enroth, *Churches That Abuse* (Grand Rapids, Mich.: Zondervan, 1992), p. 117.

✓[11]Michael Horton, *Power Religion* (Chicago: Moody Press, 1992), p. 19.

[12]*Theological Dictionary of the New Testament* (Grand Rapids, Mich.: Eerdmans, 1971), 6:3-7.

[13]Ray Peacock, *The Shepherd and the Shepherds* (London, U.K.: Monarch, 1988), p. 81.

[14]Robert Clinton, *Leadership Emergence Theory* (Altadena, Calif.: Barnabas Resources), p. 193.

[15]Stephen Arterburn and Jack Felton, *Toxic Faith* (Nashville: Thomas Nelson, 1991), p. 72.

Chapter 3: Sniffing Out the Yeast of the Pharisees

✓[1]Philip Keller, *Predators in Our Pulpits* (Eugene, Ore.: Harvest House, 1988), p. 12.

[2]F. Dale Brunner, *Matthew,* Word Biblical Commentary (Dallas: Word Books, 1990), p. 483.

[3]William Hendriksen, *The Gospel of Matthew* (Grand Rapids, Mich.: Baker Book House, 1973), p. 638.

[4]Martin Luther, *Luther's Works,* ed. Jaroslav Pelikan (St. Louis: Concordia Publishing, 1963), 26:54.

[5]Jerome Neyrey, *Paul in Other Words* (Louisville, Ky.: John Knox, 1990), p. 203.

[6]Luther, *Luther's Works,* 26:52.

[7]R. V. G. Tasker, *The Gospel According to St. Matthew* (Grand Rapids, Mich.: Eerdmans, 1961), p. 216.

Chapter 4: Heavy Loads

[1]Ayn Rand, *Atlas Shrugged* (New York: Random House, 1957), p. 436.

✓[2]David Chilton, *Productive Christians in an Age of Guilt Manipulation* (Tyler, Tex.: Institute for Christian Economics, 1981), pp. 170-71.

✓[3]Larry Crabb, *Men and Women* (Grand Rapids, Mich.: Zondervan, 1991), p. 178.

✓[4]Archibald Hart, *Me, Myself and I* (Ann Arbor, Mich.: Vine Books, 1992), p. 17.

✓[5]Bruce Narramore, *No Condemnation* (Grand Rapids, Mich.: Eerdmans, 1984), p. 301.

✓[6]Michael Horton, *Putting Amazing Back into Grace* (Nashville: Thomas Nelson, 1991), p. 123.

✓[7]Donald Sloat, *The Dangers of Growing Up in a Christian Home* (Nashville: Thomas Nelson, 1986), p. 106.

Chapter 5: They Do It for Show

[1]Anne Wilson Schaef and Diane Fasell, *The Addictive Organization* (San Francisco: Harper & Row, 1988), p. 139.

[2]Stephen Arterburn and Jack Felton, *Toxic Faith* (Nashville: Thomas Nelson, 1991), pp. 180-81.

√ [3]Gene Edwards, *Letters to a Devastated Christian* (Auburn, Maine: Christian Books, 1984), p. 5.

[4]Cited in James Beverly, *Crisis of Allegiance* (Burlington, Ontario, Can.: Welch Publishing, 1986), p. 53.

[5]F. Dale Brunner, *Matthew,* Word Biblical Commentary (Dallas: Word Books, 1990), 2:814.

[6]Ralph P. Martin, *The Epistle of Paul to the Philippians* (Grand Rapids, Mich.: Eerdmans, 1959), p. 57.

[7]Brunner, *Matthew,* p. 819.

[8]Grandma Sophie from the CBS television show "Brooklyn Bridge."

Chapter 6: Majoring on Minors and Missing the Point

[1]David Johnson and Jeff VanVonderen, *The Subtle Power of Spiritual Abuse* (Minneapolis: Bethany House, 1991), p. 138.

[2]F. Dale Brunner, *Matthew,* Word Biblical Commentary (Dallas: Word Books, 1990), 2:808.

[3]George Eldon Ladd, *A Theology of the New Testament* (Grand Rapids, Mich.: Eerdmans, 1974), p. 72.

√ [4]See Ken Blue, *Authority to Heal* (Downers Grove, Ill.: InterVarsity Press, 1987), pp. 65-88; and Ladd, *A Theology of the New Testament,* pp. 70-80.

Chapter 8: Healed by Grace

[1]Not all abusive leaders act out of a pervasive sense of shame. Some narcissistic leaders I know seem to have no conscience at all. They appear never to suffer from negative feelings about themselves. Some of them fit the description of evil people in M. Scott Peck's *People of the Lie.*

√ [2]Quoted in Daniel P. Fuller, *Gospel and Law* (Grand Rapids, Mich.: Eerdmans, 1980), p. 87.

[3]Ronald Enroth, *Churches That Abuse* (Grand Rapids, Mich.: Zondervan, 1992), p. 202.

[4]John Murray, *The Epistle to the Romans* (Grand Rapids, Mich.: Eerdmans, 1980), p. 243.

[5]Charles Hodge, *Epistle to the Romans* (Grand Rapids, Mich.: Eerdmans, 1953), p. 214.

√ [6]John White and Ken Blue, *Church Discipline That Heals: Putting Costly Love into Action* (Downers Grove, Ill.: InterVarsity Press, 1992), p. 83. (This is a retitled edition of *Healing the Wounded: The Costly Love of Church Discipline,* IVP, 1985.)

√ [7]David Seamands, *Putting Away Childish Things* (Wheaton, Ill.: Victor Books, 1982), p. 31.

Chapter 9: Healthy Church Leadership

[1]See chapter ten on church discipline. See also John White and Ken Blue, *Church Discipline That Heals: Putting Costly Love into Action* (Downers Grove, Ill.: InterVarsity Press, 1992).

[2]Gordon Fee, *Gospel and Spirit* (Peabody, Mass.: Hendrickson, 1991), p. 131.

3Cheryl Forbes, *The Religion of Power* (Grand Rapids, Mich.: Zondervan, 1983), p. 60.

4Ibid., pp. 60-61.

5George Grant, *In the Shadow of Plenty* (Fort Worth, Tex.: Dominion, 1986), p. 40.

6Thomas Smith in *Reformation and Revival* 1, no. 1 (1992): 97.

7Karl Barth, *Evangelical Theology* (New York: Holt, Rinehart and Winston, 1933), p. 12.

8John Piper, *Desiring God* (Portland, Ore.: Multnomah Press, 1986), p. 13.

9Ibid., p. 124.

Chapter 10: Healthy Church Discipline

1Ken Blue, "Interpersonal Church Discipline," M.A. thesis, Regent College, Vancouver, British Columbia, 1979.

2"In Protestant churches of the West, church discipline fell into disuse a century ago," according to Peter Breyerhous in *Dictionary of the Christian World Mission* (London: Lutterworth, 1947), p. 167. Emil Brunner concurs: "The function of church discipline has now fallen into disuse" (*The Divine Imperative* [Philadelphia: Westminster Press, 1947], p. 559).

3Geddess MacGregor, *Coming Reformation* (Philadelphia: Westminster Press, 1960), p. 17.

4John Calvin, *Institutes of the Christian Religion*, bk. 4.

5G. C. Berkouwer, *Studies in Dogmatics: The Church* (Grand Rapids, Mich.: Eerdmans, 1975), p. 375.

6These are among the points John White and I make in our book *Church Discipline That Heals: Putting Costly Love into Action* (Downers Grove, Ill.: InterVarsity Press, 1992).

7Hans Küng, *The Church* (New York: Image Books, 1962), p. 275.

8White and Blue, *Church Discipline That Heals*, p. 101.

127135